The Big Island
HAWAII
by Robert Wenkam

RAND McNALLY & COMPANY
CHICAGO · NEW YORK · SAN FRANCISCO

'Anaeho'omalu shore, South Kohala

THE RESULT OF an unusual collaboration between the author/photographer, an active citizen/conservationist; the Hawaii County government; and six large corporate landowners and developers, *Hawaii: The Big Island* is a statement of concern for the future of Hawaii Island, expressed in positive terms that recognize the fragile environment of the island and the need to preserve its natural beauty and unique lifestyle. It is an inventory and evaluation of an island's natural resources and undoubtedly presents more questions than answers. Its publication demonstrates the increasing social concerns of corporate businesses and conservationists to identify and serve the long-term best interests of the people of Hawaii. The island's scenic beauty has been recognized as not only the irreplaceable asset of a multimillion-dollar tourist industry, but also the home of more than 72,000 individual residents, who are not aware of any better place in the world to live. They like the island the way it is and wish it to remain so.

Research, writing, and photography were financed with grants administered by the Sierra Club Foundation for Hawaii County and six Hawaii corporations:

C. Brewer and Company, Ltd.	Mauna Kea Beach Hotel
Castle & Cooke, Inc.	Mauna Loa Land, Inc.
Kamehameha Development Corp.	Waikoloa

OTHER BOOKS by Robert Wenkam

NEW ENGLAND
    Text and photography by R. Wenkam
THE GREAT PACIFIC RIP-OFF
    Text by R. Wenkam
HAWAII
    Text and photography by R. Wenkam
MICRONESIA: The Breadfruit Revolution
    Photography by R. Wenkam, text by B. Baker
MAUI, THE LAST HAWAIIAN PLACE
    Text and photography by R. Wenkam
KAUAI AND THE PARK COUNTRY OF HAWAII
    Text and photography by R. Wenkam
MICRONESIA: ISLAND WILDERNESS
    Photography by R. Wenkam, text by K. Brower

Book Design by MARIO PAGLIAI

ISBN 0-528-81020-0

Contents

Acknowledgments

Norman Carlson, Kamehameha Schools Bishop Estate Land Manager on the Big Island, personally carried me by four-wheel drive pickup from the mountains to the sea—from the high summit of Hualalai to green Wai 'Ahukini beach, where the first Polynesians landed. Jan Robinson with the *Hawaii Tribune-Herald* dug into books and newspaper files for me, researching the life and times of old Hawaii. Words and music for the Hula Ala'a-papa were drawn by Neil Carlson of Chicago.

While many individuals helped me see Hawaii Island, Rex Wills II helped me hear it. A Big Island radio announcer, public relations consultant, and anthurium grower, Rex took his tape recorder on several trips around the island, visiting his friends or talking with people I suggested, recording on tape the personal commentary of island residents. His wife, Shirley Wills, asked several of her classes at Hilo High School to write their impressions of home. The book is considerably richer with these words of young and old.

Robert Wenkam
Honolulu, July 10, 1975

I have quoted from the following publications and gratefully acknowledge their important contributions to my understanding of the Hawaiian people:

Maui, The Last Hawaiian Place by Robert Wenkam, Friends of the Earth, 1970.

Hawaiian Mythology by Martha Beckwith, University of Hawaii Press, 1970. The discussion on Hawaiian gods and religion is based on Ms. Beckwith's studies. The chant "Here is the Sailing Island..." was translated by Ms. Beckwith as were the excerpts from *The Kumulipo*, University of Chicago Press, 1951.

Bishop Museum Press, 1963. Chants "The sun sends a streak of light..." and "High up in the sky...."

Fragments of Hawaiian History recorded by John Papa Ii and translated by Mary Kawena Pukui, *Hawaiian Antiquities* by David Malo (translated by Nathaniel B. Emerson in 1898), Bishop Museum Press, 1951.

Hawaii Tribune-Herald. Comments by Kamaka Paea Kealii Ai'a.

Six Months Among the Palm Groves, Coral Reefs, and Volcanoes of the Sandwich Islands by Isabella Bird, John Murray, London, 1890.

Unwritten Literature of Hawaii by Nathaniel B. Emerson, Bureau of American Ethnology, 1906. Words and music for the Hula Ala'a-papa.

Ruling Chiefs of Hawaii by Samuel Kamakau, Kamehameha Schools Press, 1961.

Journal of Reverend William Ellis, A Narrative of a Tour Through Hawaii, London, 1827.

Honolulu Star-Bulletin & Advertiser. Comments by columnist Samuel Crowningburg-Amalu and Arlo Guthrie.

Hawaii by Robert Wenkam, Rand McNally, 1972. Comments by Judge Shunichi Kimura.

Hawaii Business News. Comments by Laurance S. Rockefeller and William McReady.

Red ti in Pahoa, Puna

HIGH ON HUALALAI'S cloud-shrouded north slope, not far above the narrow belt road winding interminably between Kona and Waimea, where strings of black lava stretch downward to the sea between moats of dry grass, is located a most unusual hole in the ground. The hole is securely plugged at present; but nearly 200 years ago through the gaping vent in the earth's crust spewed a violent eruption of molten rock that flowed swiftly to the sea, forming long, wriggling strings of lava that are a characteristic feature of the now dormant volcano, as well as of its still active neighbor, Mauna Loa. The lava was unusually thin, possibly the consistency of sugarcane molasses, and flowed with such rapidity from the molten

interior that fragments of the earth's mantle from many miles below the crust broke loose from the conduit's fractured wall and were swept quickly to the surface without melting together with the basaltic lava.

Composed of almost pure minerals—silicon, iron, and magnesium—the heavy rock fragments did not become part of the lava mix flowing from the volcanic vent. The viscous magma drained away, leaving behind the extremely dense rocks from deep within the earth, which settled out of the molten lava like stones dropping to the bottom of a riverbed when floodwaters reach a still pool.

Like no other place in the world, this isolated spot on the flank of Hualalai is littered with rare specimens of the

Sailing to the Land of the Gods

earth's interior. The strange-looking rocks are out of place among the familiar pahoehoe and aa basaltic lavas. To pick one up is to grasp a peculiarly heavy weight, for they are considerably denser than ordinary surface rocks. Smash one open, and look inside for a glimpse of the beautiful glitter of a primordial semiprecious stone.

Hawaii Island testifies to the violence and power of nature, and in its volcanoes the distant origins of many of the earth's landforms are vividly revealed. The now dormant Mauna Kea is the highest mountain on earth when measured from its base on the ocean floor. Smaller Kilauea, perched on the eastern flank of Mauna Loa, is one of the world's most active volcanoes. Until 1924, when a violent steam explosion created the present fire pit of Halema'uma'u, Kilauea was a wondrous lake of molten lava attracting visitors from around the world. A permanent federal government volcano observatory is still housed on Kilauea's western rim, where the unpredictable phenomena associated with this weak part of the earth's crust are continuously observed and measured by scientists of many disciplines.

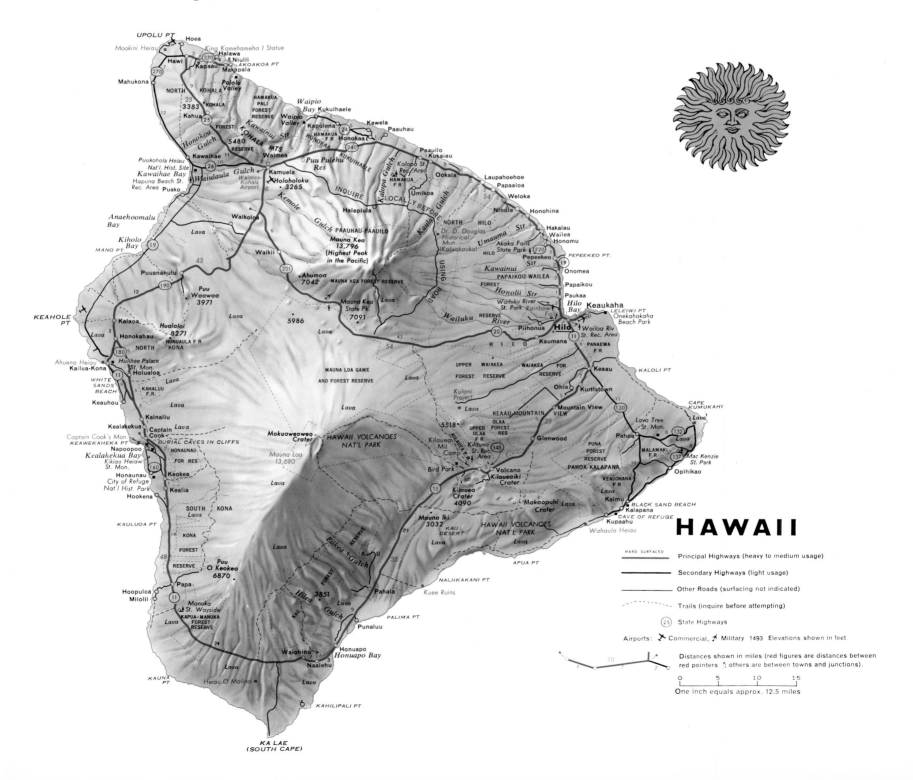

HAWAII

HARD SURFACED	Principal Highways (heavy to medium usage)
	Secondary Highways (light usage)
	Other Roads (surfacing not indicated)
	Trails (inquire before attempting)
(25)	State Highways

Airports: ✈ Commercial, ✈ Military 1493 Elevations shown in feet

Distances shown in miles (red figures are distances between red pointers ‡; others are between towns and junctions).

0   5   10   15
One inch equals approx. 12.5 miles

Over millions of years, the Hawaiian Islands were gradually built, one by one, as the earth's crust in the mid-Pacific shifted slowly northwestward over an upswelling of magma in the earth's interior. Occasionally, a fissure in the crust allowed a plume, or column, of molten rock to push upward, spilling out onto the ocean floor. In places, this outpouring of molten rock built up to such an extent that it reached above the ocean's surface and formed islands. A line of islands over 1,000 miles long on the ocean floor, beginning in the north at Midway Island, delineates the path of this plate of the earth's drifting crust as the seabed slides inexorably onward at the rate of nearly four inches a year. The molten interior, kept hot by the decay of radioactive elements—mainly uranium, thorium, and potassium—is trapped by the insulating crust, which only occasionally permits molten material to ooze out onto the surface, punching underwater mountains through the mantle as the seabed slides by.

The plumes of molten rock will undoubtedly form another Hawaiian island as the already cooled and populated islands continue their northwestward drift. Considering the inexactness of volcanology as a science, the spectacular event may possibly occur sooner than the 2 million years estimated by some geologists. Perhaps we may see the new island in our lifetime, for even now the summit peak of a submerged volcanic mountain has been plotted on the ocean floor. This seamount, southeast of Hilo, has risen to within 2,000 feet of the surface waves. On at least one occasion, a sailor on the long voyage between Tahiti and Hawaii has reported unusual, pumice-like froth floating on the ocean surface south of Cape Kumukahi, directly above the submerged extension of Kilauea's active eastern rift. Kilauea's last flank eruption in Puna poured a massive volume of new lava into the sea at Cape Kumukahi, adding about 500 acres of new land to Hawaii Island. Indeed, it should not be surprising some evening to see the red glow of a volcano reflected by clouds in the far eastern horizon. It will be the dawn of a new island.

The plate tectonics theory of continental drift helps explain the apparently arbitrary arrangement of volcanic islands in the middle of the Pacific to contemporary scientists, but early Polynesians also demanded to know the why of the heavens and the earth and evolved a theory of their own to explain the chance occurrence of these islands in the remote northeast. The basic idea behind the Polynesians' reasoning was evolved over 2,000 years ago, before they discovered Hawaii during an extended voyage of exploration to the north of the Marquesas Islands.

What ethnocentric historians disparagingly refer to as "legends" are in reality the oral history of Polynesian people, passed on over many generations by elite members of the hereditary ali'i—the chiefs—whose precise genealogies tracing their ancestry back through hundreds of years are barely matched by contemporary practitioners with a written language.

Religious celebration, which formed an integral part of the everyday activities of the Polynesians, was a continuous obeisance to gods of nature—a daily incantation of life that revolved around the sea, land, and sky. Dependent upon the earth, the Polynesians did not live on the land, but with the land. Their island lifestyle was in harmony with the sun, water, and air, and their legends spoke realistically of nature's power and influence. It was the demigod Maui, Polynesian equivalent of the Greek Hercules, who safely escorted the pioneering travelers back and forth across the trackless seas, and it was through Maui's intervention that native peoples explained the earth's behavior, whether it be the length of a day, the path of a distant star, or the location of islands.

From his grandmother's jawbone, Maui fashioned a fishhook; using his own ear for bait, Maui then pulled up many sizes and varieties of fish from the ocean. Thus he caught the islands of the Pacific, each different from the others. Then, wanting to use his mother's pet mud hen as a special bait, Maui broke off the wing when he grabbed the bird from his mother. Fishing with the imperfect bait, he caught a broken-up land—the Hawaiian Islands, which were scattered haphazardly over the sea.

In an ambitious undertaking bringing him into conflict with One Tooth, a somewhat jealous supernatural being who was already assigned the task of keeping the islands from drifting too close together or too far apart, Maui resolved to unite the islands in a single, unbroken land. Maui's mother suggested he look far offshore for help before meeting with One Tooth.

Sailing far out on the ocean to where the islands were hazy on the horizon, Maui found a calabash floating on the waves and recognized it immediately as the help his mother had directed him to find. Scooping up the calabash and putting it in his canoe, he paddled shoreward with his brothers, who had accompanied him to help pull in the catch. As they approached the islands, the calabash was transformed

This place has a lot of space energy.

Arlo Guthrie, describing
Hawaii on a recent visit

into a beautiful young mermaid, Hina, the Moon Lady. Before Maui could move toward her, the brown maiden vanished, leaving only the calabash in her place. Furious, Maui hurled the calabash overboard. The story of Maui's confrontation with One Tooth in his attempt to unite the islands is related in the author's *Maui, The Last Hawaiian Place:*

Maui's plan was to fish for One Tooth, hook him, and force him to release the islands. Maui first caught several sharks for practice, then took out his magic jawbone and tossed his line in the water. The Moon Lady, who was not annoyed at having been tossed overboard, was waiting below, and pulled the hook under without revealing herself above the waves. She carried it deep into the sea until she came to One Tooth. She approached him seductively, and One Tooth was forced to smile. He revealed his famous single tooth. Hina quickly tossed the hook down his throat when his mouth opened, then threw two loops of sennit around the lone tooth. Maui, floating anxiously in the canoe above, felt the strike. He secured the line and exhorted his brothers to paddle with all their strength. He warned them not to look back under any circumstances. The brothers paddled steadily to the northwest, but grew restless as Maui urged them on, and soon could no longer restrain their curiosity. They glanced back and exclaimed at what they saw. A string of islands—Hawaii, Maui, Molokai, Oahu, and Kauai—were caught on Maui's line and splashing along behind.

The brothers shouted, "Look at what you've caught!" The charm was broken, and the carefully placed hook slipped from One Tooth's mouth. The islands stopped in their forward movement, scattered and slipped. They churned in the water, and Kauai and Niihau spun about together near the canoe. The line snapped and hurled the others farther away toward Tahiti. But One Tooth recovered his senses in time and was able to hold Hawaii Island in place near a hot part of the ocean floor. He caught Oahu as it began to float away and, before tending to his aching mouth, stopped Molokai from jamming into the island bearing Maui's name. Maui was gone by the time One Tooth got his fish again under control, spread out much as they had been when Maui's line snapped. Not daring to take further chances, One Tooth tied them all to the ocean floor where he found them—in the places where they are today.

In *Hawaiian Mythology,* a scholarly work charting the pathway through hundreds of obscure manuscripts and articles, Martha Beckwith tells how traditional oral history was developed by the Hawaiians into a fine art with accompanying ritual and storytelling manner. A fictional story was called *ka'ao. Mo'olelo* was the narrative about a historical figure. Stories of the gods were also *mo'olelo,* distinguished by a different way of telling. Sacred stories were told only by the *ali'i* and then only during the day, and listeners were forbidden to move in front of the speaker. While the distinction between fiction and fact was not followed too closely, the intention was self-evident, and it must be understood that many so-called legends which are sometimes rejected as fantastic in actuality corresponded quite accurately with the Hawaiian view of the close relationship between nature and humans.

The Hawaiians worshiped gods of nature, gods that entered in one way or another into every aspect of daily life, played a dominant role in their history, and furnished an imaginative background for their storytelling. To the Hawaiian, any object of nature, animate or inanimate, living or dead, was *akua* (god); even a carved wood image, if worshiped as a god. Every form of nature could become *'aumakua,* or guardian god, of a family. The name *kupua* was given to the child of a god born into a family as a human being. Even the name *kupua* had naturalistic origins, coming from the word *kupu*—the young, sprouting growth. So the word *'ohana,* a family group, refers to the taro shoots (*'ohā*) that grow up about the older root.

Hawaiian Mythology goes on to explain that an appropriate animistic philosophy conditioned the Hawaiians' entire concept of nature and life, a frankly materialistic philosophy presenting none of the spiritual contradictions of Western thought. To the Hawaiians, a rock was as much a part of nature as a taro plant or human being and under the right circumstances would be worshiped with equal respect. They accommodated themselves as individuals to the physical universe—to the island environment. They did not challenge the world, but paired the opposites, one depending upon the other to complete a whole. Ideas of night and day, light and darkness, land and water, male and female appear as stylistic elements in complex chants. And although it may not be expressly stated, the opposite is always implicit, even in everyday language. This pairing determines the order of emergence in the *Kumulipo,* the amazing pre-science Hawaiian chant of creation, where from lower forms of life emerge offspring on

The old people were very healthy. Those Hawaiians down there were six-footers. They were big. I remember one time when we were outside of a store, Akaka store—that's where everybody get together to talk about things—and two people were arguing outside. They were two big men. One took the other and threw him on the roof. Hoo, they were big!

John Thomas, Honoka'a,
Born Waipi'o Valley, 1903

Hapu'u fern forest near Kilauea Iki, Hawaii Volcanoes National Park

Pololu Valley, Kohala

a higher scale and water forms of life are paired with land forms. It is the same in Polynesian genealogical chants, in which men and women are paired through literally hundreds of generations. In the *Kumulipo* genealogy it is said that the land grew up by itself, it was not created nor was it made by hand. As excerpts from the *Kumulipo* explain:

> *At the time when the earth became hot*
> *At the time when the heavens turned about*
> *At the time when the sun was darkened*
> *To cause the moon to shine . . . .*
> *The night gave birth*
> *Born was Kumulipo in the night, a male*
> *Born was Po'ele in the night, a female*
> *Born was the coral polyp, born was the coral, came forth*
> *Born was the grub that digs and heaps up the earth . . . .*
> *Born was the barnacle, his child the pearl oyster came forth*
> *Born was the mother-of-pearl, his child the oyster came*
> *   forth . . . .*
> *Born was man for the narrow stream, the woman for the*
> *   broad stream*
> *Born was the Ekaha moss living in the sea*
> *Guarded by the Ekahakaha fern living on land*
> *Darkness slips into light*
> *Earth and water are the food of the plant*
> *The god enters, man cannot enter.*

Gods are represented in Hawaiian stories as chiefs dwelling in far lands or the heavens and coming as visitors to some special region sacred to their worship. They were invoked together in chant:

> *A distant place lying in quietness*
> *For Ku, for Lono, for Kane and Kanaloa.*

The gods were recognized in the form of natural phenomena, as color, scent, clouds, rainbows and storms, the singing of birds. Some were conceived as nature deities of universal significance, like Pele, goddess of the volcano. Carved images representing the incarnation of a god played an important part in the rituals of appropriate *heiau* (temples), which were sometimes dedicated to a particular god. Other *heiau* might represent war gods, invoked by chiefs who hoped to gain special skills or victory in battle. There was even a patron god for thieves.

The Hawaiian awareness of the antithesis between sea and land, like the contrast between male and female, demon-strates the practical nature of Hawaiian worship—no opportunity for securing beneficial results from their enforced relationship with nature was overlooked. "Their imagination played with mythical conceptions of earth and heaven," wrote Martha Beckwith. "Night (*po*) was the period of the gods, day (*ao*) was that of mankind. Direction was indicated as toward the mountain or the sea, movement as away from or toward the speaker, upward or downward in relation to him; and an innumerable set of trivial pairings like large and small, heavy and soft, gave to the characteristically balanced structure of chant an antithetical turn. The contrast between upland and lowland, products of the forest and products of the sea, and the economic needs dependent upon each . . . . was recognized economically in the distribution of land, each family receiving a strip at the shore and a patch in the uplands. It was recognized in the division of the calendar into days, months, and seasons, when those at the shore watched for indications of the ripening season in the uplands and those living inland marked the time for fishing and surfing at the shore. . . . It determined the worship of functional gods of forest or sea, upon whom depended success in some special craft."

Most of the gods of the sea and forest were given Ku names, for they were worshiped as special gods subordinate to the great god Ku. Beckwith identified some of the Ku gods:

> As god of the forest and of rain Ku may be invoked as:
>   Ku-moku-hali'i (Ku spreading over the land)
>   Ku-pulupulu (Ku of the undergrowth)
>   Ku-olono-wao (Ku of the deep forest)
>   Ku-holoholo-pali (Ku sliding down steeps)
>   Ku-pepeiao-loa and -poko (Big- and small-eared Ku)
>   Kupa-ai-ke'e (Adzing out the canoe)
>   Ku-mauna (Ku of the mountain)
>   Ku-ka-ohia-laka (Ku of the *ohia-lehua* tree)
>   Ku-ka-ieie (Ku of the wild pandanus vine)
> As god of husbandry he is prayed to as:
>   Ku-ka-o-o (Ku of the digging stick)
>   Ku-kulia (Ku of dry farming)
>   Ku-keolowalu (Ku of wet farming)
> As god of fishing he may be worshiped as:
>   Ku-ula or Ku-ula-kai (Ku of the abundance of the sea)
> As god of war as:
>   Ku-nui-akea (Ku the supreme one)
>   Ku-kaili-moku (Ku snatcher of land)
>   Ku-keoloewa (Ku the supporter)
>   Ku-ho'one'enu'u (Ku pulling together the earth)
> As god of sorcery as:
>   Ku-waha-ilo (Ku of the maggot-dropping mouth)

I go hunting out Hamakua coast an' up the sides of Mauna Kea. Easy livin', peaceful . . . chee, teerreefic, that's all. Yeah, we went hunting this week, my friend and I, up Parker Ranch, and the scenery was jus' fantastic . . . Chee, boy, this is God's country. Make you feel that . . . chee, you don't want to die, boy . . . you want to stay here forever.

John Alicuben,
Hilo

Comparison of Hawaiian stories and gods with other Polynesian versions from the South Pacific provides important clues in tracing routes of early Polynesian voyagers across the Pacific. The migrations began perhaps 4,000 years ago when seafaring people from Southeast Asia launched outrigger canoes and sailing rafts on deliberate voyages of exploration to find new island homes beyond the horizon. Their discoveries were not accidental, and their accomplishments in navigation and logistics clearly overshadow the later achievements of Magellan and Cook, who sailed in larger vessels much less subject to the deep swells, crosscurrents, and seasonal winds of the South Pacific. While the Europeans were explorers amply rewarded by a short visit and satisfied to return home with simple sketches of "savage natives" and pressed flowers, the voyages of Asian peoples were made by extended family groups planning to colonize the new lands, carrying with them the seeds of edible fruits and medicinal plants, and sufficient food to eat along the way. Coconuts, breadfruit, taro, sugarcane, live pigs, and tethered birds became part of the cultural grafts for new civilizations and communities which sprang up on a thousand remote Pacific islands.

At the time Europeans were tentatively venturing beyond sheltered coastal waters to test the cold Atlantic on primitive ships that were basically large rowboats, Melanesians were sailing a familiar Pacific Ocean on swift double-hulled canoes easy to maneuver and maintain on course with the aid of unique fore- and aft-rigged sails and centerboards. Their ocean-going rafts could even be sailed more efficiently into the wind than the early square-rigged ships that carried the Europeans onto the open sea.

Over the centuries, the Polynesians evolved navigational skills allowing them to sail virtually at will across hundreds of miles of ocean without a North Star for guidance or knowledge of today's complex navigational technology. They used no compass or maps; rather, their ability to travel far beyond the sight of land derived from an intimate knowledge of the southern night sky, local winds, and currents, which enabled them to successfully return from tiny, distant islands scattered across a trackless sea they had memorized en route. The settlement of the Pacific islands is the story of great accomplishment by a civilization that thrived for 2,000 years before "discovery" by foraging Europeans who claimed the islands as colonies for their feudalistic patrons.

The islanders' sailing canoes were of advanced and ingenious design passed on orally from generation to generation by craftsmen who, because they had no written language, drafted no plans and prepared no instruction books. As the Polynesians settled in new homes across the Pacific, establishing successive communities that evolved distinctive cultures and languages, canoe design was adapted in response to new experiences and applications. But within a single island group, all the canoes exhibit identical design details typical of the cultural group. The traditions of hundreds of years at sea are reflected in the basic canoe, constructed by hand—from memory.

Long before Columbus challenged the accepted concept of a flat world by braving imagined monsters at the edge of the sea, Pacific peoples possessed a profound knowledge of the ocean and the heavens. Their complex astronomical systems enabled them to identify and trace the paths of over 150 stars visible in the Southern Hemisphere. According to geographer Gordon R. Lewthwaite, "European impact interrupted a spreading process whereby sidereal and lunar months were being coordinated, and westerners were astonished at the facile accuracy with which Caroline navigators sketched maps to oblige. Star bearings, voyaging times, and alternative landfalls were precisely indicated."

By about 1500 B.C. the Melanesians had settled Fiji. Seven hundred years later they arrived in Tonga and in another 200 years were in Samoa. Archaeological evidence indicates that 500 years later the overseas explorers had settled in the Marquesas. Before another 400 years had passed, the entire Society Island group and Tahiti had been populated, and the restless Polynesians began exploring the ocean vastness around them in an ever-widening arc, discovering Easter Island in A.D. 500, sailing on their first trip northward to find Hawaii about A.D. 600, and traveling in the opposite direction thousands of miles to New Zealand about A.D. 850. These intrepid sailors repeated their dangerous voyages with sure geographical awareness of their island world, apparently sailing at will back and forth between major island groups. The last voyage with immigrants for Hawaii probably occurred about A.D. 1200, when Samoans and Tahitians landed near Kaupo on east Maui. At the time that Europeans were engaged in the Crusades to put down Moslem heathens, Polynesians routinely completed the 2,400-mile voyage from Tahiti to the isolated islands in the north they called Hawaii.

Polynesian seafarers were undoubtedly looking for land to settle when they discovered Hawaii. In a part of the ocean so vast as the northeastern Pacific, far from known landfall

Nowadays the favorite swimming areas have been scarred or demolished. Down in Keaukaha we had this brackish water pond that we used to go and wash ourselves after surfing, but they covered almost half of it just to build a hotel that isn't even starting to being built.

Raymond Rowe,
Hilo High School

Kaimu lava shore in **Kalapana**

Mauna Kea and Keaukaha shore, Hilo

North Kona beach almost buried in Hualalai lava flow

Wilderness is *wao*, the abode of gods, spirits, and ghosts. The phrase *wao akua* means "wilderness of the gods," and implies the popular notion in old Hawaii that gods and ghosts are the chief inhabitants of wild lands.

Below the *mau* comes *apaa* (arid, dry), and below this is *ilima*, where the orange *ilima* flowers grow best. Then there are *pahee* (slippery), probably called so because of the grass growing there; *kula*, plain, open country close by villages; and the place bordering the ocean, *kahakai*, the mark of the ocean.

DIVISIONS OF THE OCEAN

Hawaiians apply the name *kai* to the ocean and all its parts. The strip of beach over which the waves run after breaking is called *ae-kai* (water's edge). A little farther out, where the waves actually break, is *poina-kai*, while *poana-kai* is the place where breakers scoop out the sand close to shore. *Kai-kohala* is the shoal water extending inward ahead of a moving wave, indicative of good surfing conditions. Beyond *poina-kai* is a narrow belt called *kai-papau*, where the water is shallow enough for wading. Where the deeper water begins is *kua-au*, and farther out is *kai-au*, the place for deep-water swimming or spearing squid.

The deep blue sea is *kai-uli* or, as it is sometimes called, *kai-malolo*, sea of the flying fish. Beyond this is *kai-hi-aku*, sea for catching *aku*, and beyond that *kai-kohala*, living place of whales and sea monsters. Beyond that is the deep ocean, *moana*, bordering *Kahiki-moe*, the utmost limits of the ocean.

When the sea is tossed into billows, they are termed *ale*. Breakers which roll in are *nalu*, and ocean currents are *au* or *wili-au*. Ocean tides are *kai-pii* (rising sea), *kai-nui* (big sea), *kai-piha* (full sea), and *kai-apo* (surrounding sea). Between tides the stationary sea is *kai-ku* (standing sea), while the ebb tide is *kai-moku* (the parted sea), *kai-emi* (ebbing sea), *kai-hoi* (retiring sea), or *kai-make* (defeated sea, the sea that died).

DIVISIONS OF THE YEAR

The year was divided into two seasons by the Hawaiians, *Kau* and *Hoo-ilo*. *Kau* was the season when the sun was directly overhead and was marked by long days; the trade wind, *makani noae*, prevailed, days and nights were warm, and the vegetation grew new buds and fresh leaves. *Hoo-ilo* occurred when the sun moved south, nights lengthened, days and nights alike were cool, and the leaves of certain plants dried up and died.

The Polynesians were aware of the 30-day month and made it their standard, a testimony to their accurate observation of the skies. The Polynesian year was regulated by the rising of the Pleiades constellation at sunset (about November 20) to mark the beginning of the *Makalii* month. The approximate length of the solar year was well known to the Hawaiians, and their months alternated between 29 and 30 days to coincide with the first appearance of the new moon in the western sky at evening.

Named divisions of the year differed from island to island. Hawaii Island's *Kau* season began with *Iki-iki* (May), when *huhui hoku* (Pleiades) set at sunrise. *Iki-iki* refers to being warm and sticky from being shut up inside because of weather. *Kaa-ona* (June) was the time when fishermen prepared *a-ei* nets for catching *opelu* and when sugarcane stalks in storage became very dry. *Hina-ia-eleele* (July) was when the fruit began to ripen; in *Mahoe-mua* (August) most of the fruit was ripe; by *Mahoe-hope* (September) sugarcane tassels appeared; and *Ikuwa* (October), the sixth and last month of *Kau*, was the noisy month with storms, high seas, and thunder.

The months in *Hoo-ilo* were *Weleehu* (November), the time when people played games; *Makalii* (December), when vines died and *kona* (south) winds prevailed; *Kaelo* (January), when destructive *enuhe* worms appeared and vines began to grow fresh leaves; *Kaulua* (February), the time when *anae* (mullet) spawned; *Nana* (March), the season when the *malolo* (flying fish) swarmed in the ocean and young birds stirred and rustled about (*nanana*) in their nests; and *Welo* (April), the last of the six months of *Hoo-ilo*, when *enuhe* worms had torn the leaves to shreds.

Perhaps nowhere in the world except the Pacific with its thousands of islands would divisions of the sparse island land, the sky, and the vast seas surrounding the islands be of such importance. The necessity for precise definitions in the spoken word produced a language admirably suited to the needs of an island people.

I like the sea. I always loved the ocean. I think the different beaches, to me, are about the best thing. I am a fisherman—mostly spearing. I go for everything—manini, kole, kūmū. I speared about a thirty-pound ulua once. Great! There's no way of explaining something like that. It's really exciting. I bent my spear around it. I use a regular Hawaiian sling— not the three-pronged type, y'know, just a straight shaft—and that thing got all twisted anyway, so I just bent it and dragged it in. This was off Miloli'i. The water is much calmer there, clearer, and there's more fish. You go to the Hilo side and it's almost all fished out. Well, we go mostly at night with underwater flashlights. We get lobster, but the lobster on the Hilo side is almost all fished out. You go to the breakwater nowadays, it's not too good. Part of it might be the cane trash the plantations put out. They used to dump that into the ocean all the time. I'm glad they stopped that practice. At least it gives Hilo and the Hamakua coast time to get back to, y'know, its original condition. I think that's a good thing. It's going to help the fishermen.

Reg Okamura, Technician,
Hawaiian Volcano Observatory

Kahua Ranch, in Kohala Mountains

Parker Ranch, Waimea, South Kohala

Mauna Kea

To me Hawaii is a much better place than most of the other islands because over here the islands aren't as crowded as it is on Oahu. The lifestyle and the ways people live here are the same ways normal people live.

Judy Ujano,
Hilo High School

Mauna Kea, Parker Ranch

Kahili ginger, South Kona

'Ohi'a lehua forest and hapu'u fern, Hawaii Volcanoes National Park

KAMAKA AI'A, the shortened form of his Hawaiian name, Kamaka Paea Kealii Ai'a, lives in the Niuli'i section of Kohala with his wife, Ester, not far from the place of his birth in 1911. When a young child in Kohala, he was among a small group of children taken to be instructed in the ways of ancient Hawaii by village elders. He remembers listening to a Hawaiian woman born in 1827 who lived to be 108 years old.

Mary Victoria Ritter, working with the Hamakua Humanities Project to stimulate interest in Big Island Hawaiiana, visited Kamaka Ai'a to ask him about his ancestors. Possessing a remarkable memory and a keen sense of detail, he speaks in the Hawaiian tradition of oral history as related in chants and *mele* by the *ali'i:*

My parents' ancestors arrived in Hawaii from different parts of Polynesia and at different times. I know less about my father's ancestors. They were of darker skin and arrived in Hawaii sometime during the sixth century. My mother was six feet, three inches tall and had reddish hair and brown eyes. Her people came from New Zealand in the twelfth century. They kept verbal records of their family history and passed them down to each generation. They lived on the southern islands of New Zealand. They were fair-skinned and were often cannibalized by the darker-skinned people who came down from the north. These people thought light-skinned people tasted better. My people would come back from fishing trips and find their people taken away. The dark-skinned people would take the lighter-skinned babies and raise them just to be eaten like *poi* dogs.

So they got together with their families and hollowed out logs to make three hundred double canoes eighty feet long which held eighty people, with a platform for provisions such as dried taro, sugarcane, sweet potatoes, papaya, pumpkin seeds, coconuts, and a type of pineapple that was long and sweet. They caught water in calabashes and stored it and other things in hollow bamboo.

They steered at night by keeping a star called *Hoku ho'okele-wa'a* between the double points of their masts and they headed for the clouds during the day. They did not know where they were going, but figured that anything would be better than what they had left. The trip took a hundred twenty-seven days.

They first sighted the southern portion of Maui; a hundred fifty left the group and headed for Maui, but the other hundred fifty, led by my ancestor, stayed out in the ocean because they thought three hundred new people in one place would deplete the land. My "father" saw the clouds over Mauna Kea and sailed on to this island. They first sighted Puako, but did not land there because they saw dark-skinned people and were afraid of them. There was a sand beach at Puako at that time. They sailed on to Kapakahi and saw more dark-skinned people, so they sailed on. They were running low on provisions, so they had to land.

They sent swimmers in at La'aumama and at Keokea. The swimmers returned saying that it looked like a good place. Then they sent runners to find out who owned the land. The runners went all the way to Ka'u before they found a *kahuna nui,* or high priest. He said they could stay if they would keep an accurate count of their population.

For years, the healthy young children were sent to the mountains to be raised so they would not have to tell him their population. They would tell the high priest that they only

I had a big stove, wood stove. My stove was as big as this freezer. It was a beautiful stove. And it had the water heater and everything inside. You want hot water, just open the door and you open the faucet and you get hot water. I used to do all my cooking, baking, and everything. It had a meter on it to tell the heat. Not too long ago, the hippies went take 'em, and they fix 'em up, because the plates from on top broke, y'know. They castings. They went broke because Danny's son went on top, y'know, and played. The hippies live up 'O'okala homestead. They bought some land up there. They took 'em and they fix 'em. And, so, they came up here one day. I still had the stove here, but I was just anxious that someone would take it away from me, because I had to move this freezer over here, and it was such an ugly thing. So, they came here one day and they said, somebody told us that Mr. Miranda is an old man and he know lots about farming, and we wanted to learn about that old farming so we could do the planting and all that. So, that day it was just pouring rain, pouring, and I told them, come in, because the rain is kind of hard. So, they came in, and they couldn't take their eyes from the stove. They were just

"My 'Father' Saw the Clouds over Mauna Kea"

had these few weak children, so he did not know how strong they were and how many people they really had.

In the mountains, they ate the things that were growing there, such as watercress, taro, shrimp, and freshwater bass. After they found these foods, they started to cultivate them. They would save the good seeds and plant them for the next generation. They fertilized the plants from compost piles that they kept.

Different things grew at different places, and they would trade back and forth. Highland taro, lowland taro, and the papayas, potatoes, and bananas were brought in by the Hawaiians at the middle elevations. They trapped the freshwater shrimp by taking the coconut fiber and pulling every other string to make a net. They made a platform and put the net up. They took the *noni* plant—the half-ripe one—and rubbed it against a rock in the stream. The shrimp would get drunk and fall into the net. The net would catch the big ones, and the small ones would fall through so they could grow big, too.

They made sandals out of *ti* leaves by weaving the *ti* leaves thick. The runners would carry four or five pairs of these shoes on their backs because they wore them out so fast. The runners traded the goods between the people who lived up high, in the middle, and down by the ocean. The people from the mountains grew and traded *pili* grass for thatching and also *kukui* bark to dye the nets so the fish couldn't see them in the water.

They made the strings from the *olonā*. It was twisted into about two or three strands. The people in the fishing villages would send dried fish and squid and squid liver up to the people in the mountains. Squid liver, or *'ala'ala nei,* was a weather indicator. They would hang it up to tell how the ocean was. If the blood was hard, they would go fishing. If it was soft, then the sea was rough.

Some fishing villages also grew potatoes and sugarcane. Sometimes they worked all night in the full moon. The women would fish for small eels. They would use small sea urchins for bait—squat down in the water and make a bowl with their skirt and put the bait in the middle, and the eels would swim in and they would catch them. Sometimes they would put the sea urchin bait in the palm of their hand, and the eels would swim in through their fingers and they would catch them.

They only grew as much as they needed until the big boats from outside started coming in and wanting to buy food. But still everyone had enough and grew very tall and strong. They raised enough potatoes to feed themselves with only a stick to dig with.

After 1865, disease wiped out most of the Hawaiians, especially those in places where the boats landed. In Kohala not as many died because it was more isolated from the outside world.

The fishing at Puako—there used to be enough for everyone—even up to twelve years ago. Now so many people fishing—they even take the fish with diapers on! Only the bottom fish left now. The fish—he hide behind the rock and peek out at me. He keep doing that, so I sneak back in from behind and rock and—bang! I got him! The old Hawaiians only had fish, chicken, and *poi* dogs for meat. *Poi* dogs taste something like mutton.

We had no flies or bugs until trade with other places started. Vancouver brought the cows and the goats. Then came the Japanese beetles and the Chinese rats and all those things that attacked the food.

looking at it. So, they asked me what kind of stove was that. And I told them it was a wood stove, but I don't use it now because it's broken and I'm going to throw 'em away. So, they didn't say a word, y'know. They went home. An' three days later they came back again. So, they say, Mrs. Miranda, if you're going to throw that stove away, you give it to us. So, I said, you take 'em. I'm telling you, the four of them and they been get one of the people around here. They had a hard time to take the stove. On the back wall was the tin and it was all rust and rotten, the same as the sink, but I didn't know the stove in the back was same as the front—all cast iron. And so, when they pulled the stove out, out came the wall and everything, an' I had to have a contractor friend up to put the house back together again. I used that stove for twenty-four years, until we got electricity.

Mrs. Manuel B. Miranda,
Kuka'iau Ranch, Hamakua,
Born 1891, 'O'okala

Hamakua pali, Waimanu Valley

Waipi'o Valley

Kiholo lagoon, North Kona

Wiliwili on Pu'u Wa'awa'a Ranch, North Kona

a month's rest, and long before that time I hope the owl-hawks will be picking his bones.

The horse has come before the rider, but Kaluna is no nonentity. He is a very handsome youth of sixteen, with eyes which are remarkable, even in this land of splendid eyes, a straight nose, a very fine mouth, and beautiful teeth, a mass of wavy, almost curly hair, and a complexion not so brown as to conceal the mantling of the bright southern blood in his cheeks. His figure is lithe, athletic, and as pliable as if he were an invertebrate animal, capable of unlimited doublings up and contortions, to which his thin white shirt and blue cotton trousers are no impediment. He is almost a complete savage; his movements are impulsive and uncontrolled, and his handsome face looks as if it belonged to a half-tamed creature out of the woods. He talks loud, laughs incessantly, croons a monotonous chant, which sounds almost as heathenish as tom-toms, throws himself out of his saddle, hanging on by one foot, lingers behind to gather fruits, and then comes tearing up, beating his horse over the ears and nose, with a fearful yell and a prolonged sound like *har-r-rouche*, striking my mule and threatening to overturn me as he passes me on the narrow track. He is the most thoroughly careless and irresponsible being I ever saw, reckless about the horses, reckless about himself, without any manners or any obvious sense of right and propriety. In his mouth this musical tongue becomes as harsh as the speech of a cockatoo or parrot. His manner is familiar. He rides up to me, pokes his head under my hat, and says, interrogatively, "Cold!" by which I understand that the poor boy is shivering himself. In eating he plunges his hand into my bowl of fowl, or snatches half my biscuit. Yet I daresay he means well, and I am thoroughly amused with him except when he maltreats his horse.

It is a very strange life going about with natives, whose ideas, as shown by their habits, are, to say the least of it, very peculiar. Deborah speaks English fairly, having been brought up by white people, and is a very nice girl. But were she one of our own race I should not suppose her to be more than eleven years old, and she does not seem able to understand my ideas on any subject, though I can be very much interested and amused with hearing hers.

We had a perfect day until the middle of the afternoon. The dimpling Pacific was never more than a mile from us as we kept the narrow track in the long green grass, and on our left the blunt, snow-patched peaks of Mauna Kea rose from the girdle of forest, looking so delusively near that I fancied a two-hours' climb would take us to his lofty summit. The track for twenty-six miles is just in and out of gulches, from 100 to 800 feet in depth, all opening on the sea, which sweeps into them in three booming rollers. The candle-nut or *kukui* . . . tree, which on the whole predominates, has leaves of a rich, deep green when mature, which contrast beautifully with the flaky, silvery look of the younger foliage. Some of the shallower gulches are filled exclusively with this tree, which in growing up to the light to within 100 feet of the top, presents a mass and density of leafage quite unique, giving the gulch the appearance as if billows of green had rolled in and solidified there. Each gulch has some specialty of ferns and trees, and in such a distance as sixty miles they vary considerably with the variations of soil, climate, and temperature. But everywhere the rocks, trees, and soil are covered and crowded with the most exquisite ferns and mosses, from the great tree-fern, whose bright fronds light up the darker foliage, to the lovely maiden-hair and graceful selaginellas which are mirrored in pools of sparkling water. Everywhere, too, the great blue morning glory opened to a heaven not bluer than itself.

The descent into the gulches is always solemn. You canter along a bright breezy upland, and are suddenly arrested by a precipice, and from the depths of a forest-draped abyss a low plash or murmur rises, or a deep bass sound, significant of water which must be crossed, and one reluctantly leaves the upper air to plunge into heavy shadow, and each experience increases one's apprehensions concerning the next. Though in some gulches the *kukui* preponderates, in others the *lauhala* whose äerial roots support it in otherwise impossible positions, and in others the sombre *ohia,* yet there were some grand clefts in which nature has mingled her treasures impartially, and out of cool depths of ferns rose the feathery coco-palm, the glorious breadfruit, with its green melon-like fruit, the large *ohia,* ideal in its beauty,—the most gorgeous flowering tree I have ever seen, with spikes of rose-crimson blossoms borne on the old wood, blazing among its shining many-tinted leafage—the tall *papaya* with its fantastic crown, the profuse, gigantic plantain, and innumerable other trees, shrubs, and lianas, in the beauty and bounteousness of an endless spring. Imagine my surprise on seeing at the bottom of one gulch, a grove of good-sized, dark-leaved, very handsome trees, with an abundance of smooth, round, green fruit upon them, and on reaching them finding that they were orange trees, their great size, far exceeding that of the largest at Valencia, having prevented me from recognizing them earlier! In another, some large shrubs with oval, shining, dark leaves, much crimped at the edges, bright green berries along the stalks, and masses of pure white flowers lying flat, like snow on evergreens, turned out to be coffee! The guava with its obtuse smooth leaves, sweet, white blossoms on solitary, axillary stalks, and yellow fruit was universal. The novelty of the fruit, foliage, and vegetation is an intense delight to me. I should like to see how the rigid aspect of a coniferous tree, of which there is not one indigenous to the islands, would look by contrast. We passed through a long thicket of sumach, an exotic from North America, which still retains its old habit of shedding its leaves, and its grey, wintry, desolate-looking branches reminded me that there are less favoured parts of the world, and that you are among mist, cold, murk, slush, gales, leaflessness, and all the dismal concomitants of an English winter.

It is wonderful that people should have thought of crossing these gulches on anything with four legs. Formerly, that is, within the last thirty years, the precipices could only be ascended by climbing with the utmost care, and descended by being lowered with ropes from crag to crag, and from tree to tree, when hanging on by the hands became impracticable to even the most experienced mountaineer. In this last fashion Mr. Coan and Mr. Lyons were let down to preach the gospel to the people of the then populous valleys. But within recent years, narrow tracks, allowing one horse to pass another, have been cut along the sides of these precipices, without any windings to make them easier, and only deviating enough from the perpendicular to allow of their descent by the sure-footed native-born animals. Most of them are worn by water and animals' feet, broken, rugged, jagged, with steps of rock sometimes three feet high, produced by breakage here and there. Up and down these the animals slip, jump, and scramble, some of them standing still until severely spurred, or driven by some one from behind. Then there are softer descents, slippery with damp, and perilous in heavy rains, down which they slide dexterously, gathering all their legs under them. On a few of these tracks a false step means death, but the vegetation which clothes the *pali* below, blinds one to the risk. I don't think anything would induce me to go up a swinging zigzag—up a terrible *pali* opposite to me as I write, the sides of which are quite undraped.

All the gulches for the first twenty-four miles contain running water. The great Hakalau gulch which we crossed early yesterday, has a river with a smooth bed as wide as the Thames at Eton. Some have only small quiet streams, which pass gently through ferny grottoes. Others have fierce, strong torrents dashing between abrupt walls of rock, among immense boulders into deep abysses, and cast themselves over precipice after precipice into the ocean. Probably, many of these are the courses of fire torrents, whose jagged masses of *aa* have since been worn smooth, and channelled into holes by the action of water. A few are crossed on narrow bridges, but the majority are forded, if that quiet conventional term can be applied to the violent flounderings by which the horses bring one through. The transparency deceives them, and however deep the water is, they always try to lift their fore feet out of it, which gives them a disagreeable rolling motion.

We lunched in one glorious valley, and Kaluna made drinking cups which held fully a pint, out of the beautiful leaves of the *Arum esculentum*. Towards afternoon turbid-looking clouds lowered over the sea, and by the time we reached the worst *pali* of all, the south side of Laupahoehoe, they burst on us in torrents of rain accompanied by strong wind. This terrible precipice takes one entirely by surprise. Kaluna, who rode first, disappeared so suddenly that I thought he had gone over. It is merely a dangerous broken ledge, and besides that it looks as if there were only foothold for a goat, one is dizzied by the sight of the foaming ocean immediately below, and, when we actually reached the bottom, there was only a narrow strip of shingle between the stupendous cliff and the resounding surges, which came up as if bent on destruction. The path by which we descended looked a mere thread on the side of the precipice. I don't know what the word beetling means, but if it means anything bad, I will certainly apply it to that *pali*.

A number of disastrous-looking native houses are clustered under some very tall palms in the open part of the gulch, but it is a most wretched situation; the roar of the surf is deafening, the scanty supply of water is brackish, there are rumours that leprosy is rife, and the people are said to be the poorest on Hawaii. We were warned that we could not spend a night comfortably there, so wet, tired, and stiff, we rode on other six miles to the house of a native called Bola-Bola, where we had been instructed to remain. The rain was heavy and ceaseless, and the trail had become so slippery that our progress was much retarded. It was a most unpropitious-looking evening, and I began to feel the painful stiffness arising from prolonged fatigue in saturated clothes. I indulged in various imaginations as we rode up the long ascent leading to Bola-Bola's, but this time they were not of sofas and tea, and I never aspired to anything beyond drying my clothes by a good fire, for at Hilo some people had shrugged their shoulders, and others had laughed mysteriously at the idea of our sleeping there, and some had said it was one of the worst of native houses.

A single glance was enough. It was a dilapidated frame-house, altogether forlorn, standing unsheltered on a slope of the mountain, with one or two yet more forlorn grass-piggeries, which I supposed might be the cook house, and eating house near it.

A prolonged *har-r-r-rouche* from Kaluna brought out a man with a female horde behind him, all shuffling into clothes as we approached, and we stiffly dismounted from the wet saddles in which we had sat for ten hours, and stiffly hobbled up into the littered verandah, the water dripping from our clothes, and squeezing out of our boots at every step. Inside there was one room about 18 x 14 feet, which looked as if the people had just arrived and had thrown down their goods promiscuously. There were mats on the floor not over clean, and half the room was littered and piled with mats rolled up, boxes, bamboos, saddles, blankets, lassos, cocoanuts, *kalo* [taro] roots, bananas, quilts, pans, calabashes, bundles of hard *poi* in *ti* leaves, bones, cats, fowls, clothes. A frightful old woman, looking like a relic of the old heathen days, with bristling grey hair cut short, her body tattooed all over, and no clothing but a ragged blanket huddled round her shoulders; a girl about twelve, with torrents of shining hair, and a piece of bright green calico thrown round her, and two very good-looking young women in rose-coloured chemises, one of them holding a baby, were squatting and lying on the mats, one over another, like a heap of savages.

When the man found that we were going to stay all night he bestirred himself, dragged some of the things to one side, and put down a shake-down of *pulu* (the silky covering of the fronds of one species of tree-fern), with a sheet over it, and a gay quilt of orange and red cotton. There was a thin printed muslin curtain to divide off one half of the room, a usual arrangement in native houses. He then helped to unsaddle the horses, and the confusion of the room was increased by a heap of our wet saddles, blankets, and gear. All this time the women lay on the floor and stared at us.

Rheumatism seemed impending, for the air up there was chilly, and I said to Deborah that I must make some change in my dress, and she signed to Kaluna, who sprang at my soaked boots and pulled them off, and my stockings too, with a savage alacrity which left it doubtful for a moment whether he had not also pulled off my feet! I had no means of making any further change except putting on a wrapper over my wet clothes.

Meanwhile the man killed and boiled a fowl, and boiled some sweet potato, and when these untempting viands, and a calabash of *poi* were put before us, we sat round them and

Mauna Loa summit

Makalawena beach, North Kona

Taro fields, Papala Falls, Waipi'o Valley

Akaka Falls State Park, near Hilo

GEORGE LANAKULA KEIKIAHI NAOPE is a *hula* instructor and entertainer. Born in Honolulu on Oahu, he moved to the Big Island on his fifth birthday to live at the family's Hawaiian homestead in Keaukaha. Director of the Council on Hawaiian Heritage, he heads his own program to teach island children of all races the rich heritage of song and dance passed down from ancient days. Financed by the State Foundation of Culture and the Arts, his *kulana naua'o* classes have attracted more students than they can handle—one class has 60 students. But George Naope is not one to compromise, insisting that every student learn to beat the *ipu* (gourd drum) and to chant—and know the story and meaning of the dances. In Hilo, Naope commented on the *hula* and Hawaiian entertainment:

I was raised by my *kupuna*—my great grandmother. She never spoke any English at all. She died when she was a hundred and nine years old and I lived with her. Her name was Malia Naope, and she did everything. She was a royalist, really. She just opposed everything that was foreign to Hawaii, even the foreigners themselves. She was a lady-in-waiting to Queen Liliuokalani and she revered the *ali'i*. She loved her heritage especially, and I guess a little bit of it has rubbed off on me. She was very fond of the ancient chants, especially, and this is where I got most of my knowledge. . . . The *hula oli* [chants] are the history of Hawaii. Our people didn't have a written language, but the Hawaiians had good memories and they passed their history on from generation to generation.

For years the *hula* was *kapu* in Hawaii, right after the coming of the missionaries. The masters of the *hula*, thank goodness, they practiced in the villages, secretly, because of the influence of Christianity in Hawaii. They kept it all secret—the *hula kapu*—until Kalakaua became king of Hawaii. And King Kalakaua, who was a composer and author and lover of Hawaiian folklore, said that he thought the *hula* was the language of the heart and therefore the heartbeat of the Hawaiian people. And King Kalakaua is credited with reviving hundreds of dances at his coronation in Honolulu. And these have all the histories of the different islands. He brought out all these master teachers, who were in hiding and just teaching on the side, to bring the very finest of their dances to Oahu to participate in this revival of the Hawaiian art of dance and chanting. That's why many of the *mele* or chants that you hear today have the ending in the words *na he i noa no Kalakaua*—it means "long may he live," "long may his name live"—because he revived many of these dances. So they always say, "*He i noa Kalakaua*," thanking him for reviving all of these dances, 'cause the *hula* was stopped in Hawaii for so many years.

We have one chant I know that tells of this island. It is called *E, 'Ike Mai*, and it tells of the land that the creator created and what he put on the island of ours, like the birds and the flowers and the forests and, y'know, many other things that we have on Hawaii. Anyway, this is an *oli*, really, not a chant where you dance standing up. It's a sitting kind of dance:

I luna la, i luna	Above, above
Na manu o ka lewa	All birds in air
I lalo la, i lalo	below, below
Na pua o ka honua	all earth's flowers

I enjoy the land up at Pohakuloa. The land is dry, though here and there you will find patches of green grass. Despite that, many beautiful flowers grow. I think the cool air helps, because if it were sunny and hot all the time, the flowers would wither and die. At night it can become very cold, but because I prefer cool places from somewhere like Hilo, it doesn't bother me as much as it does others. I really feel carefree and as though everything's going smoothly with my life when I'm up there. It's dusty and rocky, but it's also cool, and when I'm up there I can look down and see part of the island and its nature. When I see all that, I wish the world could be mine.

Jewelle Sanbei,
Hilo High School

"The 'Hula Oli' Are the History of Hawaii"

I uka la, i uka	inland, inland
Na ulu la 'au	all forest trees
I kai la, i kai	seaward, seaward
Na i'a o ka moana	all ocean fish
Ha 'ina mai ka puana	sing out and say
	again the refrain
A he nani ke ao nei	Behold this lovely world

I think tourist business is good for Hawaii. They bring us a living. But I feel—and I hope nobody will get insulted if I say this—but I don't think that the *malihini* are getting exactly what they should be getting. And in this I am talking about entertainment and particularly Hawaiian entertainment. You know, many people have saved all their lives, they dream about coming to Hawaii. Save all their money and they come here expecting to see Hawaiians—Hawaiian culture, Hawaiian music—which in the hotels we do not have. It seems that rock and roll is the kind of thing that the hotels like. Maybe because they're making money off it, I don't know. But I talk to many *malihini* here who come to see our Hawaiian show, and they all say that this is the kind of show that they come to Hawaii to see. And we do a strictly Hawaiian kind of show, and I myself never gear my show to the *malihini*. In other words, I don't Hollywoodize it, like in those Polynesian mixed-up shows, because I feel my first obligation is to my people, and as long as I feel I can please my people—you know, our people here, our local people—then I think the mainland *haole* will love us.

I don't know why, but my show was the only Hawaiian show in Hilo. I put it on at the hotel only once a week because I didn't have the time—and maybe too much Hawaiian blood! I don't think the cost is the problem. It just seems the managers of the hotels . . . It depends on the manager: If he digs Hawaiian stuff he's going to have Hawaiian things; if he feels this other kind of entertainment is bringing in money, I guess this is the purpose of them having the hotel, you know. . . . There isn't a Hawaiian show in Waikiki, no way. They have good Hawaiian singing, maybe at Halekulani—they're trying to keep all of these old Hawaiian traditions together—but nobody pushes the Hawaiian show anymore. The only time you get to see a good Hawaiian show is probably when you go out to the rural area or get invited to a baby *luau*, and then you see all the Hawaiians out there, and it's a ball. And this is what the *malihini* lose, y'see. They don't have the contact anymore with the locals. This is the top of anybody's vacation, to meet the local people, and very few of our local people patronize the hotel establishments, unless it's somebody real great that they want to go and see. . . . I think if you had a real Hawaiian show every night in Hilo, you'd have tourists every night to see the show. Those people who venture over here, especially those that come from the mainland and other places, they come here because they love Hawaii and they want to know everything about Hawaii. These are the ones that really push Hawaiiana, not the Hawaiians themselves, because maybe the Hawaiians feel they know enough about it all. But it's the *malihini* who get involved with Hawaiian people, involved with Hawaiian things. They kind of gave up everything and came here to live, and they're the ones that push the program because they believe that this is what everybody in Hawaii should learn.

Although it has been partially accomplished, it is necessary that we further determine the carrying capacity of our land for various and appropriate uses. In doing this, long-range decisions would be based on what the land can handle, with the amount of environmental degradation kept at a minimum.

Establishment of an optimum population for Hawaii is inevitable. As people realize the environmental and social degradation associated with continued population growth ad infinitum, the natural growth rate will stabilize. In-migration to Hawaii will also stabilize as work opportunities come into balance and the visitor industry more carefully prices its product to attract a quality clientele. If we understand the carrying capacity of our land, we will be better able to cope with growth and determine to what extent orderly development can be accommodated in years to come.

Judge Shunichi Kimura,
Third Circuit Court, Hilo

Bamboo orchid, Puna

Bamboo orchid

Vanda orchid hybrid, Hilo

Oli and Mele from the Hula Ala'a-papa

Oli – Prelude

Arranged by Mrs. Yarndley

Ha -láu Há -na-léi i ka ní -ni a ka ú -a; Kú -má -no (i) ke

pó' -o-wái a-(a-a) ka lí -ko; Na há ka ó -pi-wái o Wái - a-ló -ha (e)

O ke ká'-he kó'-e a hí-ki i Wai - ó' - li. Ua í-ke - 'a, (e).

Mele no ka Hula Ala'a-papa – Chant

No - lú -na ka há-le kái, e ka ma' -a-lé -wa, Na ná ka má-ka

(Anticip.)

ia Mo - á -na-nú -i -ka-Le-hú -a. Nó -i aú i ke kai (la) e ma-

tremolo.   tremolo.

li' -(-i - i) -o.   Á -ne ku a'e la he le -hu -a i-lá-i-

(New breath.)

-(i - i - i) -la,   (i - i - i -i,)   Ho - pó' -e Le-hú -a-

(Anticip.)

kí -e - kí -e. Ma - ka'u ke ka-ná - ka i ka le-hú -a, (he) Lí-

lo i-lá -lo e hé-le ái e-(-e - e - e), i-lá - (-a)-

- lo,   e-(-e-e-). Ké'-a-aú i-li- í--li né-he; o-(o)-lé-lo, ke-

-(e) kái o-(o) Pú-na I ka ú -lu há - la la, é'-(é - é),

(4 times r.)

kai- ko'-o Pú - -(u -u)-na, (e -e -e - e). la hó'-o-né'-e-né'-e

ia pí - li mai ká - ua, (la -a), E ke hó - a, ke wái -ho

(Anticip.)

e mai la ó -e; É - ia (e) ka mé -a í -no, he á-nu, ě-

-(e - e - e.) A - ó-he á-(a - a - a)-nu, e -(-e - e - e - e.)!

(Anticip.)

Me he mé-a la i-wá-ho ká-ua, e ke hó-a, Me he wá-i la ko ká-

ua í-(i - i - i -i-i -)-li, (e - e-e-e - e-e - e - e).

CHANT FROM THE HULA ALA'A-PAPA

From mountain-retreat and root-woven ladder
Mine eye looks down on goddess Moana-Lehúa.
Then I pray to the Sea, be thou calm;
Would there might stand on thy shore a lehúa—
Lehúa tree tall of Hopoe.
The Lehúa is fearful of man,
Leaves him to walk on the ground below,
To walk on the ground far below.
The pebbles at Keaau grind in the surf;
The sea at Keaau shouts to Puna's palms,
"Fierce is the sea of Puna."
Move hither, snug close, companion mine;
You lie so aloof over there.
Oh what a bad fellow is Cold!
Not cold, do you say?
It's as if we were out in the wold,
Our bodies so clammy and chill, friend.

In Hawaiian words of the chant, the stress accent is placed
over syllables that take the accent. A word or syllable italicized
indicates a drum or gourd downbeat.

Mauna Kea summit, Mauna Loa lava flow

Pu'u Pua'i cinder cone, Hawaii Volcanoes National Park

BORN IN 1815, Hawaiian historian Samuel Kamakau, like David Malo, received his higher education at the Lahainaluna Seminary on Maui. Encouraged by one of his missionary teachers, Kamakau began to take a scholar's interest in the history and traditions of his people. Kamakau's work, published in English translation as *Ruling Chiefs of Hawaii,* covers Hawaiian history from the earliest chiefs, known only through tradition and legend, to the death of Kamehameha III in 1854.

In his chapter on the death of Kamehameha III, Kamakau brings out the Hawaiians' insistence on the importance of education:

He [Kamehameha III] attained to the ruling power [in 1825] when he was but eleven years of age. . . . In his speech at Honuakaha he proclaimed "The government of learning" in which chiefs should teach commoners and each one teach another. Teachers were distributed about the islands, and only those who could not walk stayed away from school. Some schools had a hundred, some a thousand pupils. From children to bearded men, all were gathered into the schools. Buildings went up over night to serve as school houses; if a landlord refused to build he lost his post. A line separated those who could read from those who could not. The concert exercises by which they were taught delighted the people. The rhythmical sound of the voices in unison as they rose and fell was like that of the breakers that rise and fall at Waialua or like the beat of the stick *hula* in the time of Pele-io-holani and Ka-lani-'opu'u.

A ea mai ke kai o Waialua,	Let the sea of Waialua rise,
Wawa no 'olelo 'oko'a i pali,	Let the roar echo over the hills,
Nunu me he ihu o ka pua'a hae la,	Rumble like the grunt of the wild pig.
'Ako ka lau o ka nalu pi'i i ka pali,	Let the rising wave break the leaf from the cliff.
Ku pali Kaiaka i ka 'ino,	Kaiaka cliff stands above the storm,
'Ino ka lae o Kukuilau'ania,	Stormy is the cape of Kukuilau-'ania,
He Maka-nui.	Windy indeed it is!
Makani me he ao la ka leo o ke kai,	The voice of the sea rises upon the wind
Kuli pa'ia wawa ka uka a Lihu'e,	Deafening those in the uplands of Lihu'e,
O me he 'oka'a la i ke kula,	As it is borne over the plain,
Ke kula hahi a ke kai e halulu nei,	The rumbling of the sea treading upon the plain.
Halulu ma ke Ko'olau,	Rumbling over Ko'olau,
Ho'olono 'Ewa,	'Ewa hearkens,
'A'ole i 'ike i ka po ana a ka nalu,	She has not seen the rising of the waves
Kuhihewa wale no Wahiawa-e.	And mistakes it for Wahiawa.

The Hawaiians' considerable respect for knowledge is compared to the miracle of nature in a chant inspired by missionary teachers during the rule of Kamehameha III, who had declared, "My kingdom is a kingdom of learning."

Nani na lehua kapili wai a ka manu,	Beautiful is the *lehua* where birds are snared,
Nani na lehua lu lehua a ka manu,	Beautiful the *lehua* scattered by the birds,

"My Kingdom Is a Kingdom of Learning"

Nani na pua o ka a'ea'e,	Beautiful are the blossoms of the a'ea'e,
Nani na 'ulu hua pala i ka lau,	Beautiful the ripened breadfruit among the leaves,
Nani na ki 'owai o Kalawari,	Beautiful are the pools of Calvary,
Nani wai o ua nei i ka pali,	Beautiful are rain-filled pools in the hills,
Paku aku la i na pali,	Hidden from sight among the hills.
Hio na lua o na wai i ka makani,	The wind blows shaking the dew from the leaves,
Noho paku i ke kuahiwi,	Of the close-grown thickets of the mountain.
E ho'i ma Hiku i ka uka,	The month of Hiku returns to the uplands
Ka lala i ka wai la ku'ua,	Where the rain forms streamlets,
Ku'ua mai manu'u kelekele	Streamlets that swell into rivers
Ho'okelea mai e ka la,	Sparkling in the sun.
O Maku'ukaokao, o Makilihoehoe,	Here is Maku'ukaokao, Makilihoehoe,
Ka lala i ka na'auao la ku'ua,	Whose learning flows like a stream.
Ho'onu'u iho a ku kahauli.	Eager these to be honored men.

Though he acknowledged the cruelties of some of the old laws and practices, Kamakau still felt something had been lost with the passing of the old ways. In *Ruling Chiefs of Hawaii* he wrote:

In old days people who lived in out-of-the-way places were heavily burdened by labor performed for chiefs, landlords, and land agents. But although the work was hard, that today is even more so when families are broken up and one must even leave his bones among strangers. In the old days, the people did not work steadily at hard labor but at several years' interval, because it was easier then to get food from the fishponds, coconut groves, and taro patches. Hogs grew so fat that the eyelids drooped, bananas dropped off at a touch, sugarcane grew so tall that it leaned over, sweet potatoes crowded each hill, dogs fattened, fish cooked with hot stones in the early morning filled the food gourd, and a man could eat until he set the dish aside. This was the generous way of living under a chief who made a good lord; the people were fed and every wish of the chief was gratified. Labor done in the patch of the chief was a rental paid for the use of the land and everyone was benefited thereby. Today the working man labors like a cart-hauling ox that gets a kick in the buttocks. He shivers in the cold and the dew-laden wind, or broils in the sun with no rest from his toil. Whether he lives or dies it is all alike. He gets a bit of money for his toil; in the house where he labors there are no blood kin, no parents, no relatives-in-law, just a little corner for himself. In these days of education and Christianity there is no regard for the old teaching of the ancestors. In those days the boys were taught to cultivate the ground and fish for a living, the girls to beat out tapa and print patterns upon it, and to work well and pray to the god, and they were taught that it was wrong to be indolent and take to robbing others. These teachings were held in esteem in old Hawaii, and the land was rich and its products varied.

I've been all over the world and in many, many great places, but I don't think there is any place like Hawaii, and when I say Hawaii, I mean our island of Hawaii. Even in comparison to Oahu. I like to go down there 'cause it swings, but there's nothing like coming home to Hawaii. For some reason or other, Hawaii instills me with all of the aloha, for all the history of Hawaii is here in this island, and my mana'o—thinking—is on this island. I can't explain it, y'know, but all that I know about Hawaiiana I received on this island. And because we have on this island any kind of weather that you like, the climate, y'know. If you want cold climate you can go to Waimea, or you can go to Volcano. If you want nice, sunny beaches you can go to Kawaihae. We have Kona. Anything that one desires in a place is here on this island.

George Naope,
Hilo

Hibiscus, Hilo

Pandanus and coconut, Kaimu beach, Puna

Hale-o-Keawe heiau and ki'i in City of Refuge National Historical Park

City of Refuge National Historical Park

Hawaiian petroglyph

Hoʻokena, South Kona

Halema'uma'u eruption in Kilauea crater, Hawaii Volcanoes National Park

Kilauea eruption on east rift, near Kapoho, Puna

'Ohelo growing in pahoehoe lava, Mauna Loa

Steaming spatter cones, near Pahoa, Puna

Sunset at Kauna'oa beach, South Kohala

Francis: *First wife, no kids. Second wife, no kids. The kids here are hers.*

"Who's this big girl?"

Leilani: *That's my number three girl. That's my daughter. That's her little girl that's running around. She calls my husband and I Daddy and Mummy. Here, try some of this. That's* uhu-*fish.*

"OK if I use my fingers?"

Francis: *Like the old people say, if you eat with one spoon you just like one horse—you get the bit in da mouth. You know how they tell you, you wasn't born with a spoon and a fork.*

Leilani: *He caught that at Kiholo, and the uhu was so-o fat that the liver part, that's what we mixed up! That's the first time I ever taste it like that, y'know, with the liver all mixed up. I said, "Chee, it taste just like it get 'inamona inside, doesn't it?"*

Francis: *That's the leevah.*

Leilani: *That's the liver from the fish.*

"Now that you are sort of retired and have a young wife, what do you do?"

Francis: *I in charge of Kiholo land for the Hinds and Carlsmiths.*

Leilani: *Mos' of the time we're down Kiholo, and we just come up* mauka *to feed our animals, and like me, I got to have my house cleaned up, and then we go right back again.*

Francis: *Tomorrow we going.*

Leilani: *We cannot leave until after lunchtime 'cause the gas man has to come up fix my dryer.*

"Now you have a dryer!"

Leilani: *Fifty years ago we didn't have any.*

"What did your mother do about washing clothes?"

Francis: *Well, to tell the fac', I'm not shame. Those days, y'know, dis Eagle brand, for bag flour, y'know, the forty-nine-pound bag flour, eh, and it had an eagle, huh? Those days, after they use the flour, they went bleach 'em. When they bleach, they dry 'em up in the sun, use soap. But those days we not use the white soap, they have the brown soap—a long block.*

Leilani: *We used to call it the brown soap.*

Francis: *Yeah, the old one, y'know.*

Leilani: *That's the kind my mother used to wash our clothes, and if she's going to bleach it out, you use that soap, and by God, the clothes came out nice and white!*

"How did they wash?"

Leilani: *Board and brush.*

'Ōhelo berries

"Where did you get the water?"

Francis: *Brackish water.*

"How about drinking water?"

Francis: *Rainwater. Well, we keep the water. We catch the water in a wooden tank.*

Leilani: *It's the same thing like we have now. We don't have any pipe—wai, y'know, a waterline—so, whatever we have is from the rain. We do have a line now that runs down from the ranch for the cattle, so we can just jump in, in between and connect up the pipe and come in here, but most of our water comes from rain. If we have plenty rain we have plenty water.*

"When you were a kid, Francis, what kind of stove did you have?"

Francis: *We have that regular Hawaiian stove—firewood. We make a few stones and pipes.*

"And you ate rice?"

Francis: *Very seldom we ate rice, 'cause we raise taro, too. We make our own poi, my father pound poi. I was too small.*

"How about salt?"

Francis: *Well, salt, when rough time the sea go over the banks and you get a little pond here and there. Tha's where we get the salt—save 'em up.*

"Sugar?"

Francis: *Oh, sugah. We get the brown sugah, the washed sugah they call 'em, from the store.*

"Who owned the store?"

Francis: *Chinese, Ah Kui. Every month you pay.*

"So, your father got paid from the ranch and the fish, and your mother from the lau hala hats, and the kids had to work, too?"

Francis: *Everyone gotta work. You gotta go strip the* lau hala *for make the hat, for help my mother pick the* lau hala.

"And how did she fix the *lau hala?*"

Francis: *Well, first you get from the pandanus tree, cut the pick, you know where is that? On the end cut 'em. Peel off two ends with your finger, then roll in your hand. To cut 'em we have stripper—lau hala stripper make from any piece sheet iron. Make 'em sharp. File 'em down. Too bad, I no more my strippers. I show you the strippers. I went give away all of mine.*

"What was good about being a kid?"

Francis: *Ah, I don't know, but the only thing is, I'm proud that I learned erryting from my father and my mother. Teach me what to do an' that, y'know. They told me you gotta learn erryting. When we're not here, you on your own. You know how you going to live.*

"They meant like learning to fish?"

Francis: *Fishing and then how to cook your own and erryting. I have long nets. I have throw net.*

"What was breakfast like?"

Francis: *Well, those days we have pancake made from flour and coconut juice and fry 'em on top the outside stove.*

Leilani: *Y'know, in those days, and in fact, I remember when we used to come over to stay with my grandparents, pancakes was famous in the olden days.*

"Did you use any shortening?"

Leilani: *Ah, the only way then to get lard was, y'know, when they killed the pig. The fat, they used to boil that, and render the fat, and that's how they got their grease. And to save it, they just put it in a bowl and it keeps; and it stays on the side, and whenever they want, they got a little wooden spoon where they used to dig into this bowl. And everything used to be mostly put in a crock. Hawaiians used to call it kelemania'ai. Big ones for the poi. They had all different size crocks. And I used to see when my grandparents used to do that, my mother used to be there. But pancake was famous. And the part of it that I used to enjoy about it was when it was guava season. Every time when it was guava season, we know we're going to get up and, like we call it now, cowboy pancake. It's r-e-e-al thin. It's only flour and baking powder is used in that, with a little salt, and you mix it up with water. And what my mother and grandparents used to do was, after they got it all fried up into pancake, they used to sprinkle brown sugar in there and they put jelly in it and they rolled it up.*

"Like a crepe suzette."

Leilani: *That's it, the same thing. And that's what Hawaiians used to do, and they were famous for that.*

"You used a lot of coconut, too?"

Leilani: *Yeah, the coconut milk. That's what they used to use for milk to cook the lū'au, the taro leaf. Then we ate the 'a'ama and the small white crab.*

"Did you get lobster then?"

Leilani: *Not now.*

Francis: *Any seacoast today is nothin'. They wipe 'em all out.*

Leilani: *'Opihi [mollusks]. Wana [sea urchins]. Just eat it. Just like that. I like it just like that. In fact, that's the only way you can eat it, and if you leave that standing up too long it just melts by itself.*

"Did you eat raw fish? How did you fix it?"

Our environmental and recreational resources are finite. It would be foolhardy to think that we can accommodate more and more people without incurring any costs to our physical environment. . . . All of this makes the necessity of a population and growth policy even more pressing and critical. We can no longer afford to let growth continue at an unshackled rate without first having a greater understanding of its tangible and intangible ramifications. We cannot afford to have a "growth for growth's sake" mentality guide our decisions.

Raymond Suefuji,
Planning Director,
Hawaii County

Koa acacia, Waimea

Koa off Mana road, Mauna Kea

Francis: *With salt.*

Leilani: *No lemon juice or anything, just salt, strictly Hawaiian salt.*

"How about chili pepper?"

Leilani: *Yes, that was put in, too, but for the children they used to separate the chili pepper ones. I know my grandparents used to do that. They claimed that chili pepper was no good for the eyes—*

Francis: *You use too much chili pepper, oh, you get tears come up from your eye errytime. . . . You see like our place over here. The younger guys when they go fishing they gotta use glass.*

Leilani: *Ah, Polaroid glass.*

Francis: *For see the fish.*

"Well, how did you find them in the old days?"

Francis: *Eye 'nuff.*

Leilani: *Up to today, even his grandson Francis Hao lives down here. He comes up, he looks at me, "Auntie, looka tūtū-man," and he's out there throwing net. He says he can see the fish, but I can't see the fish without my eyeglasses. He has to have that Polaroid glass. Even me sometimes. I look at him and I say, "Chee, I don't see any fish." But when he throws the net, he brings the net up, there's fish in it.*

"When babies came along, Francis, when you were a kid, with no hospital—"

Leilani: *Who helped your mother when she gave birth?*

Francis: *The oldest one, my father, the community come give us some help.*

Leilani: *I remember my mother. I was the oldest, and in all she had eight children, but there were only five had survived. And when it was time for her to give birth, my dad was the only one. He stood by.*

"There must have been something done to protect the baby."

Leilani: *I was old enough to see where my mother had to go through birth at home. I was born at home, and my dad was there to help her, and he was the only one. When the baby came out, he was there to cut the cord off and tie it and he was there to—*

"Who taught him, Lei?"

Leilani: *Well, I guess it must have been through the family.*

Francis: *Generations.*

Leilani: *Generations, I think. So, the only thing, I had seen that, and the first thing he did after she gave birth was to take care of the baby, cut cord, wiped the baby up, and they had this coconut oil, that's what they used. They rub on the baby. Afterwards he put the clothes on, wrapped it up in blankets, put the baby aside, and then he went and attend to my mother. Where you would call the afterbirth. When that all came out, then he would pick it up, wrap it up, and he would go outside, dig a hole, deep, and bury it and covered it and that was it.*

Francis: *Sometimes they give 'em leeker, huh?*

"How about liquor? Did your dad have liquor?"

Francis: *Yeah, dey get da kine—ugh—Hawaiian swipe. I don't know how they make 'em. I don't know why they give. They say for pīwa [fever] and for wash all the blood out, or what, I don't know.*

Leilani: *But my mother had never taken anything like that. All I used to see, my mother would sit up, dirt was on the floor, see, and after my dad had taken care of the baby, then he would come right behind her back and with his two hands just rub around like this, you know, on her 'ōpū [abdomen], and everything would just shoot out. And then he would carry my mother up. He would wipe her up. Those days I used to see where they had this old white sheet. Now we got Kotex and whatnot. In those days no more. Had this clean white sheet, and he would put it around her and he would dress her up, change her clothes and everything, carry her on the bed, and then he would clean up all that afterbirth . . . I didn't see my father boiling water or anything. In fact, my mother had given birth to my youngest brother when we were in Ke'ei. I think the baby came way ahead of time and there was nothing prepared. So there was no fire, but my dad knew what to do; and the only thing I remember, there was a bottle of coconut oil which they made themselves, and he got that oil and he rubbed it on the baby, and that's how the baby got cleaned, from that coconut oil. Then he would use a clean cloth like a rice bag, and he would tie the string on the piko [umbilical] cord. I asked him if I could help, but he said, "No," in Hawaiian, "you kids just stay outside."*

"When you got sick with no doctor, what did you do?"

Leilani: *I know, for myself, we never had any doctor. My mother took care of us. But the famous medicine in my house was castor oil and enema. When she knew we were coming down with a cold, that was it. And another, that you call it today, was steam bath.*

Francis: *Steam bath the bes'.*

Leilani: *But in those days they call it pulo'ulo'u. They had this big tub of hot, steaming water, and they'll cover you all up with a blanket, and they go out and pick up 'clyptus leaves and throw it inside this bucket of hot water.*

I always interested in animals. My dad was also cowboy himself for the old Parker Ranch. He started with Carter, Mr. Carter in Kamuela, and I always been working with my dad. It is really hard work. If you like it, you take interest in it very much. It's a rough life, outside in the rains. You always out on the go, steady with the animals all the time, makes you more richer with life as a cowboy.

Thomas Kaniho,
Seamountain Ranch,
Ka'u

"Did you ever use *noni* or *pōpolo* leaves?"

Francis: Popolo *is, so far as I know, for baby. They chew the popolo after they rub it on top the head.*

Leilani: *We used to have that, even the leaves make a tea. And another medicine that my mother used to give us was a brown—it looked like dirt.*

Francis: 'Alaea?

Leilani: *Oh, I used to hate that. Boy, if she knew I had a temperature or sompin' like that, she'd get that, boy, go get that. I think one teaspoon. She'll mix it up with water and she'll make us drink that right down. Oh, I used to hate that. Down Laupahoehoe side used to have that, because my tutu-man used to go get the stone and come home and pound that with the poi pounder. It used to come in little chunks. He used to pound that until it gets into fi-i-ne—almost like dirt—and then they just pick it up and put in a bottle and store it. That was their medicine.*

"Francis, what kind of parties did you have when you were little?"

Francis: *Very seldom they have* luau *down Ke'ei. The only game they play was the older people play tug-of-war. The kids play, too. . . . Had parties, but not too much like now when you have baby* luau *and get all kine for eat. But those*

days they hardly could afford to get erryting, see. Of course, they have kalua peeg, yeah, they raise their own peeg.

Leilani: *My grandparents used to raise pig, but the pigs they raised were inside the coffee patch. They had papaya trees and whatnot. My grandparents used to send us kids out into the coffee and call the pigs home, and each one of them had their own names, Hawaiian names, y'know. They used to answer the calls. I don't care how far they are, they'd come back. And my grandfather had a box where he had cooked this taro with banana and papaya all mixed up. You call one pig, everyone comes.*

"Some people feel they have everything in the city—how about you?"

Leilani: *Well, let's put it this way. Outside of the ocean, even though it is so far away, we do have everything. We have a good life. The reason I say we have everything here is because we got the land to live on. We can do as we please. We can plant what we want. We have two acres now. We raise our own vegetables, which I think is very important today because when you go down to the market—cabbage, onions, well, vegetables alone are very expensive. The pigs that we have here now are all wild pigs that we have caught, down the beach. Some of them we caught, just babies. We have one*

Breadfruit

Hawaiian petroglyphs at 'Anaeho'omalu

Coconut palms at Kalapana, Puna

particular one now, which we call 'Ehu. My husband caught that one. Just a little baby. He catch it by running after and just catch it with his hand. We raised him for two years now. I don't think we could ever kill that pig—that pig is so tame that you go up there and say, " 'Ehu, you go to sleep, now." She'll look at you, "Oink-Oink." The third time you tell her, she just lays right down. If she wants petting, she'll tell you she wants petting, though my brother in Hilo wouldn't believe it until he seen my husband do that. . . . We have chickens, ducks, pigs, sheep, cattle—six head. We used to slaughter, but now I want it packaged, so we take to Andrade, at Ahualoa. . . . We kill the chicken.

Francis: I catch him and I cut his neck.

Leilani: We all pitch in and do the plucking. Here in Pu'uanahulu we are so far away from everything. I feel that this little community here is really isolated. There are about fourteen families. Altogether the amount of people would be about fifty.

"How did you get this land?"

Leilani: It's from the Hao, his first wife. This is the way I understand that the families here in Pu'uanahulu got their property. Uh, konohiki?

Francis: Konohiki, yeah.

Leilani: Way back from before the olden days, many Hawaiians came here and they were told, well, you claim so much of this and you claim so much of that property, and from then each generation passed on down to their children are carrying it out.

"What does Pu'uanahulu's name mean?"

Francis: Pu'u means "hill." Ana means "cave." Hulu means "feathers."

Leilani: Right in back of us is called Pu'uhuluhulu. Right behind here, there's a little field you know as, well . . . Anytime when you go towards Kona, on the way coming back, you know that hill where the bulldozer has defaced—it's being pushed over? Well, right up there it's called Pu'uhuluhulu. Over here we're noted for many 'o'o—the bird with the yellow feather that chiefs made their capes from.

"Do you ever see that bird anymore?"

Francis: No more—even the 'i'iwi no more, now.

Leilani: But during Hind time, he says they used to have that. We have wild turkey by the dozens. I have people who come up here and they want to buy them. I look at them, I laugh. I say, "No, we don't own the turkeys." "Well, where do these turkeys come from?" "They're wild turkeys." "You must be kidding." I say, "No, I'm not." They're all over the place. They roam up here. They eat my chicken feed. That's OK. They even jump inside the pigpen. We don't bother them.

"Why don't you catch them?"

Francis: The taste is funny.

Leilani: Well, according to the people here, the bird is too tough. But if you caught them and raised them by grain, then be all right. It's the same thing with the wild pigs.

"What do you feed the wild pigs?"

Francis: Grain and coconuts. We get the coconuts down the beach.

"Did they make kūlolo when you were a kid?"

Leilani: Well, the kūlolo was made underground in the imu. We mixed taro and coconut into a pudding. But the haupia, I used to see my grandparents make that on the outside stove. It was nothing to them. It was drop in the bucket, as you would say. It was nothing. You should see them when they do that. They have a grater—handmade. They sit on this board, and they would grate the coconut. Then maybe they have a bowl filled up. They pass it on. The next one gets it, start squeezing. It was more like a teamwork. The families would be there if they know you're going to make kūlolo today. For those days to make haupia they didn't have cornstarch. It was a Japanese starch. It comes in a long, white, skinny bag and it had a Buddha on it, and that's what they used to use for their cornstarch. And that's what they used to use also for poi, you see, in order for them to spread the poi out. They go out and they put two or three package of this starch and boiling water. They would cook this starch in there, stir it up, and it comes out just like Jell-O. Then they wait until the starch is cooled off. After it's cooled off, they pour it into the crock of poi and mix it up, and then your poi would raise up.

"When your father pounded poi, did he put it through a cloth or something?"

Francis: No, no. He used a stone and poi board. Just kept pounding.

Leilani: Sweat and all goes inside that taro. I used to do that. When it came time. When I used to see my mother and my dad pick taro, I know already time for pound poi. They used to cook the taro first, and when that taro is cooked, you put it aside and start peeling that skin off. After that skin is all peeled off, they put two, three taros on the board. They have a long board, and one sit the other end, one sit here. They have a bowl of water on the side. They stick their hand in that water and they put a little bit on the taro and onto the stone and you start pounding. Keep going—pound and pound—

Let me tell you that when I first moved here, one night the door slammed, and I thought I had locked the back door. The next night the same thing happened—it opened up and slammed shut. Madame Pele? Well, my garage didn't have any windows, and when the wind blew, naturally what had to give was my back door in the garage. I found out that my house was built over a crack, so whenever Kilauea crater swells, so does my house. It all separated very silently, but it did. And so the doorjambs didn't match and the locks didn't fit in. So what happened is, just before an eruption when the volcano swelled up, the house opened up. And the wind blew and it would come into the house, and everybody said Madame Pele had come to visit and bless me.

Al Pelayo, Manager,
Volcano House

until that thing comes out real smooth. Every lump had to be down, y'know, and if that lump isn't down, you can't get away from that board. I used to grumble, "Oh, who going come relieve me?" You hear the old folks talk in Hawaiian. My dad and my mother spoke strictly Hawaiian to us at home, and they used to get awfully angry with me when I didn't speak Hawaiian. So I used to turn around and tell them, "Look, we go to English school." I could understand when you speak Hawaiian to us, but for me to answer back—I couldn't do it. I used to have to ask back in English, and that used to annoy them. Very much.

"Sitting here, looking at the top of Hualalai . . . Did you ever go up to the top?"

Francis: *Yeah.*

"What's up there?"

Francis: *Nothing.*

"Any Hualalai legends?"

Francis: *Only the blowhole. That's when you go there—beeg hole, y'know. The wind come from under.*

Leilani: *Even like over here in Pu'uanahulu, mauka behind here, down there by the roadside, there's trees growing there. Cows go in and out there. There's graves all over in there, ancient graves. They have some up here . . . ancient graves, makai side. Ancient graves. As you go down the old road going down to Kiholo, what they call that?*

Francis: Ka hale moekolohe.

Leilani: *Means "house of fool-around," "house of play-around." Well, the story to that is, if someone wanted to run away without anyone knowing that they're going together, there was one place down here, and this old lady used to take care of that place.*

Francis: *Two old folks.*

Leilani: *Yeah. Husband and wife.*

Francis: *They hide them two people over there. The old road come through there, the guys finding for their daughter and son. The people stay finding for it, they come through there and they ask. They went see that boy and the girl gone. They say no, but they were hiding them inside their house. 'As why they call that place is* ka hale moekolohe.

Leilani: *Even down to Kiholo now, there's hole still stand till today, that cave. You have to climb down with a rope and a stick, and it's in between the new road and the ocean now. And in that cave they have a canoe—a half of a canoe.*

Francis: *Two small head inside one small kind trunk.*

Leilani: *Y'know in 1956 when these two* haole *men had left the island here and were on their way back to Honolulu*

on their plane, and it blew up in the air? Well, those two had left here, and they were the ones who had took all the combs and the things that they used for fishing out of that cave there. And on their way back to Honolulu, the plane blew up in the air before they landed. When that happened, the people here at Pu'uanahulu knew that they had taken that, because they were taken on the tour, y'know, of the place. And they found this cave and they just picked up all this things, and they were warned not to take them. But to them it was something, so they just took it. So, when that accident happened, the people here claimed that they were being punished for taking things. Now, even after today, we have a cave, but not here. You go in there and you see a lot of skeletons, y'know. But those skeletons were there long before whoever this people who are living now. But their parents and their grandparents had already told them, don't disturb the graves but leave them alone. But they have a lot around here, even down Kiholo.

"Maybe Pu'uanahulu at one time, with water, was a very important place?"

Leilani: *It was, way back at one time. This little district here was noted for ali'i. Used to stay here traveling. This was their resting place.*

"Who's the oldest resident of Pu'uanahulu?"

Leilani: *He is, right here.*

Francis: *But me, I'm only a newcomer. I married a Pu'uanahulu girl, that's why. But all the old people all dead already.*

Leilani: *And even if you go ask anybody about the Hinds, even if you were to talk to Bobby Hind, he would tell you go talk to Francis Ah Nee. Because he had worked with his grandfather, the father's grandfather, right down to Bobby's time. Francis was Mr. Leighton Hind's boy. Every place Mr. Leighton went, Francis was there. Even out fishing and everything. . . .*

"Thank you very much. I could talk with you for weeks."

Francis: *Well, drop in anytime when you come. Maybe I find some more history.*

Leilani: *No, no. You're not taking our time, because this is good when you find somebody that's interested.*

Francis: *Bring your wife and we can spend a day at Kiholo, and we show you all the old places.*

Leilani: *They got the eight ponds. It's water clear as crystal and you put your finger in—sweet. You can see the bottom. It's beautiful.*

•   •   •

I like this island very much, but the only thing that I dislike about it is that there is too many tourist coming here. This is what is destroying this island, because with the tourist there will have to be more planes coming and this brings air pollution. And plus they will have to build hotels and then they have to take down the natural things just for this hotel. If I had my way, I would say no people from the mainland can step foot on our Hawaiian Islands.

Jo Ann Katano,
Hilo High School

Painted church at Honaunau, South Kona

Bougainvillea and African tulip near Pahala, Ka'u

Puna highway

Change Is Coming

HERBERT MATAYOSHI, the mayor of Hawaii County, which comprises all of the Big Island, expressed his concerns and hopes for the future of Hawaii and its natural beauty:

I'd like to see the lifestyle of Hawaii Island being kept as much as possible in a rather rural atmosphere. So I am stressing quite a bit the agricultural field for development of economic opportunity. I think by so doing we can keep a lot of our lifestyle here, without the massive concrete jungles, giving the people the chance for open space *and* job opportunities.

I really believe we can develop the visitor industry without destroying the environment. I see this, because for the visitor industry to remain viable, and continue to grow, we must preserve our natural beauty. We must have more regional parks and recreational areas both in the mountains and along the shore. And outdoor opportunities for families. As we provide a better life for our own residents we will also offer the best possible opportunity for visitors to enjoy our natural environment. If we were to mutilate our natural environment, I think we would also destroy the visitor industry. . . .

I don't like to see our visitor industry built on such things as horse racing or gambling. This is why I say visitor industry growth is very compatible to preservation of the environment. I think the various natural resources and the beauty of the island are what will sell. I don't think we need gambling to attract people. We'll leave that to the other states that don't have the natural beauty we have.

We have the plans to regulate orderly growth: the general plan, the zoning plan, the height limitations, the density—height to open space, setbacks on the shoreline, setback from the property line, minimum lot size, and so on, so there is some control. We have regulations for water, shoreline protection—this is all in the books, and I think this is very good. There are other possible controls—like bulk control. The building could be of lower height, but larger size. Aesthetics come into it. One thing is parking space, for instance. . . . As I say, I don't know yet how to control it all, but control it, the kind of growth, we must.

There's more concern now for the future, with planning. There's much more desire for planning. I think there's a lot of recognition of the speed with which things are changing. There is a great emphasis on planning and goal setting and what we ought to be trying to achieve, like what kind of island do we want? What kind of lifestyle? Goals could be in terms of preservation as well as development. There is a growing concern and awareness among people for the future of our island.

Looking back, I guess you can reminisce a little bit. Where I guess we all didn't have enough money. Everything was really at kind of a slow pace, where you could ride your bikes and move around wherever you please. Now we've gone to a little faster pace, cars, roads . . . and I suspect that in the future it will continue to change as rapidly because the jets are coming in with the new terminal, the visitor industry, agriculture—all growing. But to keep the old atmosphere of Hawaii, I think it is necessary to keep the economy of this island essentially agricultural; and these are our efforts here, to give the island a rural atmosphere and keep the lifestyle about the same, recognizing at the same time there is change coming.

I think the island of Hawaii, hopefully in the next decade and a half or two decades, will certainly be the best place to live—if it's not already. I figure that it is, and we want it to stay that way.

The improvements we seek are incremental; they do not flower overnight.

John A. Burns,
Former governor of Hawaii

89

Wai'ahukini green sand beach near Ka Lae, Ka'u

'Ohi'a lehua, Ka'u

'Ohi'a lehua forest and anthurium, Puna

ROBERT YAMADA is chairman of the Hawaii County Council. A self-made businessman and successful politician, Yamada was born in 1909 in a plantation camp at Papa'aloa on the Hamakua coast. At his office in the Yamada Trucking Company, Hilo, he recounted the rags-to-riches story of his last half-century on the Big Island:

I did not work on the plantation, but my father had worked there, and they really did have a hard time. My sister got a homestead in Manoapae, in Laupahoehoe, and we moved there when, I believe, I was about five, six years old. From there I attended school, and my mother raised vegetables—truck farming. I lost my mother early. She was a hardworking woman, very small, and she peddled all the vegetables that we raised to the other plantation camps.

There were eleven kids in the family. I came number four, the oldest boy, which made it very tough and difficult for me, because it's an oriental custom where the first son of the family usually takes over all the problems. . . . With eleven in the family I don't think our parents were able to accumulate any wealth working for about thirty or forty dollars a month in those days. And my father was a hardworking man, too, but never did accumulate any wealth, so we kids had to help work.

At the age of thirteen, that's when I lost my mother; my father was still in his middle forties. . . . Anyway, I did go to school, no mother, and the family was all broken up. So at the age of sixteen, I was attending Hilo High School on the train that ran down Hamakua coast at the time, but my father won't give me any train fare, so I was ducking the conductor every morning and every afternoon. When the conductor pass I'm in the toilet, or, you know what I mean, eh? Or I go running around so he wouldn't collect ticket from me. But then I got fed up dodging the conductor. I had enough, so at age sixteen I quit school. When I quit it was only about one month from graduation.

My father had quit the cane-growing business and he went into trucking. He had a one-ton truck. After a couple of months he says that's not for him and he wanted to quit. Coming home from school on the train, I had to help my father deliver the freight after I got home in the country. You gotta deliver all the freight until eight o'clock, nine o'clock, and in the morning I had to get up to catch the train to go to school. I said, "Doggone it, I don't think I can stand this anymore." So when he said he quit, I took over the business on one condition—that I pay all the bills. So I did pay all his bills. And then he went into the taxi business after that. So, he did his taxiing and I was in the trucking business. And that's my beginning at the age of sixteen. I could hardly carry a hundred-pound bag, but I did. I really worked. I think I worked about sixteen to eighteen hours a day. Driving from Laupahoehoe I used to make sometimes two trips a day to Hilo, and remember, now, that's the old winding road, not the new road. It was a Dodge one-ton truck, and flat tire I used to get. We used to overload, y'know. I used to sit down and pray no flat tire! I was that desperate. But anyway, with that truck we went on and bought some more trucks and so on.

I was nineteen years old when I married my wife, Emma. You see, her adopted brother used to work with me. He was only sixteen or seventeen, a kind of smart boy, but he didn't like schooling, so he started working with me. So naturally I go to the house, right? Pick him up in the morning, and then in the afternoon go back to his house to deliver him. And his auntie, or my wife's auntie, was such a *nice* Hawaiian woman. Then I start going there, and first thing you know we got together, so she and I got married. She was only sixteen. My wife is Hawaiian and part Portuguese.

I now have three children. Two boys and one girl. They're all grown up and have a family. My daughter is forty-six, my son forty-five, and I have another son forty-two. They're all with me. Everyone. My daughter is chief clerk in the office,

The changing values of society are expressed in the ecology movement, the youth revolution, and the revolt against materialism—good old Christianity has been saying that for years—and all of this is having a wholesome, restraining effect on our use of land and natural resources. We are beginning to see that the needs of people as a whole are escalating in relation to the needs of the individual. . . . I am referring principally to profit. The carte blanche-laissez faire kind of enterprise which built this country would tear it down if allowed to go unchecked. We've already had 200 years unchecked, and we are rapidly using up our nonrenewable resources. . . . This system of ours is about to reprove itself. We will not throw away our marvelous economic triumph. Men will overcome pollution of the environment and at the same time learn to enhance their environment. The people who are already clamoring to make that happen may need to be a little more patient, but they must not be less determined.

Laurance S. Rockefeller,
Owner-builder,
Mauna Kea Beach Hotel

"Make Them Feel the 'Aloha' Spirit"

and my oldest son running my rock plant. You know, rock-crushing business. My youngest son runs my contracting business.

As of today, although I started as a trucker, and that was my main business, well, you probably know, if you live in a small community like Hilo, you get to a saturation point in no time, and I wasn't satisfied with that. So gradually I got into land development business. My sons were all growing up, and I had always thought how am I going to provide job for myself. My youngest son was a good Cat skinner, a good tractor operator, y'know, and my oldest son can also operate heavy equipment. My daughter went to commercial college, that's a business school. She went there and she came back and worked for us since she started, and she still working for us. And we diversified those days to contracting. My son went to college for two years and he got fed up with school, too, and he said he's going to come home and work. So he came back and started working, and now he's running the contracting business and his son is also helping him. I kinda treat them nice as much as I know how and what I can afford. So I have all my kids, my wife, my two brother-in-laws, and three grandsons working for me. I now have about a hundred and sixty-five employees, including supervisory and rank-and-file.

The first time I got into politics was in 1957. I used to be Democratic county committee chairman and I supported candidates strongly. I had a pretty good trucking business, and I did a little contracting and so forth—always had a few dollars in my pocket. I thought that now that I made a few bucks, I should do some service for the people. Really, you know, it sounds very corny, but I really thought if I was elected maybe I could do something. And that's how I ran in 1957. I got elected with one of the biggest votes ever had in those days to the board of supervisors.

At that time, Jimmy Kealoha was the chairman. Because I was too aggressive, I guess, and I'm not the kind of guy that plays petty politics just for the vote, he and I got into friction, because, more so, I had the courage enough to raise the fuel tax. The fuel tax is still on yet. The reason why . . . In those days, the county employees was working eight days a month, and I can't see me making a living working only eight days a month. So I said, well, it's high time that the people of Hawaii should pay a fuel tax and from the fuel tax hire these people, give them twenty-one days, one month's work. Keep them going. So I did that, and we had some leftover money, so we paved roads from Keaukaha to Kona. In those days you can stretch the money, y'know. If you get four hundred thousand dollars it's something like three million dollars today. You could really stretch, and our salary was only two hundred and fifty dollars. But sometimes I got in problem with Jimmy Kealoha, and he's the chairman. He was a very popular chairman, he'd campaign and kiss everybody's baby and kiss the wife. But I'm not that way, I'm just the opposite. I'm serious, you know, and I didn't want to play politics either. But anyway, I got so mad because some of the projects which I started, he goes around and said that he's the one that made it. But I worked hard to get the money. But he's the administrator, so he goes out with the engineers and he got all the credit. So I said, "To hell with this," and I ran against him. Everybody told me don't run—if you run for the board you'll be in the next ten, fifteen years, as long as you want to. But I ran knowing that I didn't have much of a chance against him. But I thought this was a good way to face up, so I ran, and I lost. I didn't run again until the charter was amended so I didn't have to run every two years, and to my surprise, after being away from office eight years, I came in number two. And I got elected after that again.

Y'know, no county will go broke, because you can always up the tax to balance the budget. However, if the people don't elect people that are very concerned, only elect because of their popularity or because they're a female, or they're

The Beeg Island before bettah, yeah? Now, not so good. All the trees destroy, eh? You go in this area. Only papaya tree now. The forest once bettah. The forest moah nice, eh? Free. Plenty avocados in the mountain before. Plenty to eat the year round you get. When they knock down now, they knock everything down, so they no leave the good stuff up, yeah? Everybody doing now. They knock the old and the new ones out. That's why the land look barren nowadays. No more the old trees. You go up Pohoiki—all wipe out, yeah? Bettah leave some old ones around, y'know . . . too late already. Da kine beeg trees—why they push 'em down for?

John Hale, Puna resident,
talking about clearing land
to grow papayas

Hapu'u fern on Hualalai, North Kona

Honaunau Bay, South Kona

Japanese or Filipino or Portuguese, and disregard the quality of the people, we may have problems as far as balancing the budget. As long as we are prosperous like the last three years, during Mayor Shun Kimura's time, everything is all right. That's the best time in the history of the county of Hawaii. Things were growing and growing. Subdivisions and money coming in and buying. The more people buy, the more they develop, the more revenue we have, so the more we can spend, right?

The future, I believe, will be bright providing we approach it very cautiously, especially with the spending during a recession period. And then we should liberalize some of the development. Not be too stringent. And forget about government later subsidizing things like improving the road or streetlight or sidewalk. I think we should develop to give everybody the opportunity to come in and spend so they can contribute to the support of the county. I really and truly feel that there's

a good possibility that this place will develop into one of the finest counties in the state of Hawaii.

To show you, look at all the money I have. I'm still investing it at my age, because I find that everything is going to appreciate in value. Sure, we may have some kind of a depression or recession for a certain period, but in that case you act accordingly and spend accordingly. Then when the good time comes, you're there.

I was born, reared, and I made a good living here on this island, and I'll be proud to be buried here. I think this is the best place to live. I can say this, probably, because I don't have much experience or knowledge of how the living and life is any other place . . . I haven't been to any other place outside of traveling. But I can observe other places. And I come back here and the friendliness of the people here, the opportunity that we have here if your eyes are wide open and

Coconut grove near Honaunau, South Kona

you're a little bit *akamai* [wise] . . . There's such an opportunity over here if you got a few bucks. I can't see living *any* other place, and I'm very happy, and I want all of my family to live here and make their living.

This is an island where you can't forget about the tourist industry, because we're depending on tourists and agriculture. We got no other business that we can explore at the present time. Of course, we have a little fishing, a few flowers, and so forth; sure we have all of these, but the major industry is tourists and big agriculture. I'm talking about big revenue. People get job opportunities and tax revenue for the county. The future depends on tourists and agriculture, right? So, we have to concentrate, and I think we have a good opportunity to perpetuate the tourist industry providing the people here are concerned about the tourists and try not to take everything away from these people. Make them feel at home. Make them

feel the *aloha* spirit. Make them feel happy that they came here. The government will also have to provide something for them in the area of recreation, entertainment, and make them feel also proud that they visited the county of Hawaii.

I think to a certain degree the government is aware of this, but I don't think we are doing enough. To what extent these people expect service from the government, I really don't know because I cannot look at myself as a tourist. But knowing what exists, what I feel for these people, most of them are very happy and want to come back again. My biggest worry is how *long* can we perpetuate this feeling of *aloha*. If we develop and the town becomes like a mainland city—I don't know, maybe we might lose this sense of *aloha*. We'd probably be like any other place, but it won't take place in the next twenty years. I think Hawaii will be Hawaii for a long time to come.

Construction site in Kailua-Kona

Mauna Loa and Hilo Bay

Hybrid orchid, Hamakua

Kealakekua Bay, South Kona

Kiholo beach, North Kona

Hawaiian petroglyphs at Puako, South Kohala

locality for the accommodation of travelers but a crazy old grass hut and a Chinese cook." The Volcano House of 1866 boasted four bedrooms, a large parlor, and dining room. Management claimed they could shelter 20 persons for the night—with a certain amount of sharing. The roof was grass-thatched.

In later years, tourist hotels would not rest so gently upon the land, and while sugar mills and cane fields changed the appearance of the island, the rural beauty was retained. It was not until engineers began building straight and monotonous highways up the Hamakua coast to handle bulk sugar trucks that postwar economic development began to seriously alter the island landscape. Tourist industry demands further hastened construction of unsightly roads where none should have been. Following Hawaii statehood, the lava wilderness of North Kona was opened for potential development with construction of the Queen Ka'ahumanu Highway from Kailua-Kona to Kawaihae.

Often praised as a "clean, non-polluting" industry by its advocates, tourism was labeled quite differently by conservationists after the National Park Service blasted a highway through the remote Kalapana lava fields so tourists could drive more conveniently through the national park from Puna, using the Chain of Craters scenic road. A provident lava flow, undoubtedly instigated by Pele, the volcano goddess, promptly covered over the mistake. State highway officials pushed another "improved" highway through Honaunau pastures to the City of Refuge National Historical Park, gouging out scenic vistas en route to provide a "safe alignment" for bulky diesel tour buses. Screaming jets flying off extended airport runways drowned the old tranquility of Hilo. Obnoxious advertising and sellers of plastic leis and glass beads despoiled the most significant historical sites, while tourists crowded public beaches and bargain tour groups split hamburgers for lunch. Discovering Hawaii's delicious lifestyle along with the tourists were enterprising developers intent on exploiting the island by selling it at their highest price.

The renting and selling of Hawaii Island to overseas immigrants is only one of the recent activities to significantly alter fragile island ecosystems and expose the earth and culture to decay and deterioration. The inherent contradictions involved in tourism make it mandatory at this late date in Hawaii's history that careful thought be given to all aspects of the island's unique environment, if only to preserve Hawaii's greatest remaining assets—its natural beauty and cultural differences.

Unspoiled land offers the greatest tourism potential. It seems to promise to civilized people the fulfillment of their dream of getting away from it all, of starting all over again—a carefree life on a virgin tropical isle with year-round sunshine, orchids, and brown maidens. It is the implied theme of tourist advertising, yet each visitor to Hawaii injures a little of this fragile land, not only for himself, but also for every visitor to follow. To accommodate unlimited visitors is to destroy much of the treasure they came to enjoy, for overdevelop-

ment is antithetical to conservation since it is synonymous with resource exploitation. With every new construction there inevitably is destruction of natural values. The history of Hawaii is testimony to this immutable fact.

Exponents of unrestricted growth and progress seem to think they can ignore the limitations imposed by nature. While more cautious citizens suggest careful study of the problems of continued growth without limit—however orderly that growth might be—the developer's bulldozer continues to rearrange the island landscape. The bulldozer can shove nature around, but the developer cannot ignore nature, because nature has a way of shoving back.

Improved sugar harvesting techniques on Hamakua coast plantations in years past netted planters greatly enhanced yields, but the more efficient processing of cane poured tons of silt into the sea, wiping out baitfish and the island's commercial fishing industry. The hasty building of a concrete seawall along Kailua's shore to protect the county road forced a change in ocean wave patterns, destroying the largest beach in Kona.

Nature always laughs last. We are reminded by every decision that scars the earth that we must in final analysis live on earth's terms. If we want a beautiful island—a livable island—with a remunerative economy in future years, we must make it so by rational and thoughtful decisions based on nature's restrictive terms—not ours. If we intend to invite visitors to share our land, we cannot go on trying to maximize their numbers and our profits. The carrying capacity of the island as determined by our needs for open-space recreation, clean air, and agriculture must be the determinant of the island's optimum population. Over the short term we can grow fat and rich if we wish to duplicate Las Vegas or Miami—but we will destroy our way of living, and our island in the sun.

But mainlanders from every state still clamor for escape to Hawaii. The South Pacific paradise implied in every advertisement is still the end of the rainbow. The soft landscape of sensuous hills in Kohala is forever green; the waterfalls of Akaka bright and clear; volcanoes give visual evidence of a spiritual rebirth; every day in Hawaii is a wonderfully sleepy Sunday. Winter weeks are *aloha*-shirted, short-sleeved summers.

Of course, the problem is one of determining how many tourists can be lodged on an island without destroying the very environment they came over 2,000 miles to share, and still leave space and beauty for the people who call the island home.

How many people can live on an island? There cannot be a hotel on every beach, a road to every volcanic summit, a condominium tower on every skyline. To allow entry for every visitor able to afford a ticket will ultimately destroy this island treasure. At some moment, at some time very soon—perhaps sooner than we would like—the people of Hawaii Island must advise the potential visitor, "No more reservations are available—the island is full."

Miloliʻi, village in South Kona

WHEN FIRST sighted from the deck of a low-hulled sailing schooner still 24 hours from port, or from an airliner three miles high and five minutes out of Hilo airport, Hawaii Island seems to be floating among the clouds. There is no color separation where sea and sky meet on the horizon. The island appears to hover quietly in that space between the earth and sky which ancient Polynesian seafarers called *lewa lani*—the place above where the birds fly. The gently sloping flanks of Mauna Kea and Mauna Loa sharply etch the lower edge of the sky, outlining the narrow place for human habitation with seasonal whitecaps of snow. The island is more within the sky than upon the sea.

The sky occupies the space remaining after the volcanic summits take their share, smoothly outlining infinity and sporadically puncturing the blue island roof with complimentary red squirts of molten lava that splatter back upon the earth. The endless lava flows squirming downward off the huge hulk of Mauna Loa and Hualalai are like the entrails of some prehistoric monster oozing from the inner earth.

The cold lava of a hundred eruptions lays upon itself in thin sheets of rock outlining the island where ocean waves rest against the wet shoulders of ancient mountains, ending their long journey across the sea. Waves tentatively touch the shore and retreat again and again into the ocean before rising in foaming swells, their white crests swirling in the wind like wild horses' manes. Then, sweeping swiftly and determinedly across the glistening beach, they disappear into the sand.

Windward, the sky of clouds is full of motion and change, constantly pushing squalls of rainbow showers toward the shore. The green carpet of sugarcane is monotonous and still, disturbed only by the invisible push of trade winds bending cane tops into earthbound waves. The swishing cane tassels of Hamakua are silver whitecaps on a stormy green sea.

Narrow threads of white water cling briefly to the sides of Waipi'o, falling in random steps onto the valley floor. The slowly growing stream twists back and forth in a nomadic path to the ocean, where incoming waves wait impatiently on the black sand to carry the river joyfully away, like young lovers eloping into the sea. At the end of day, the misty walls of Waipi'o absorb the light of sun and clouds, merging day into night; mountaintops disappear into the darkness. The fading light of evening reveals the proscenium of the universe outlined by stars against the light of space.

It could be the description of another world instead of the island within our reach. It is testimony in rock and water to nature's ability to create beauty, providing trees, flowers, and birdsong in just the right places, fashioning a landscape so uniquely beautiful there can be no copy. An irreplaceable island—the only one of its kind we have.

We are all interlopers upon nature's domain and unfortunately not always aware of the shortness of our visit on earth. Whether we were born on the island or are simply visitors stopping by, all of us are transients and should be more responsible for the land during our brief tenancy.

Given time, nature has the ability to hide the worst mistakes of man beneath tropical jungle growth or rampaging lava flows. In recent years, tsunami waves generated thousands of miles away in Alaska and Chile swept the decaying Hilo waterfront clear of commercial litter, creating the most beautiful oceanfront of any community. Visionary planners had for years failed to initiate action. Nature did it overnight.

Hawaii Island still exhibits the exposed scars of perhaps 90,000 subdivided lots, carved by speculative developers in years past who carelessly subdivided lava flows seemingly before they cooled, pushing cinder roads into tree-fern jungle and orchid-strewn grassland.

"Own your own land in Hawaii," echoed the irresistible spiel of glib salesmen in mainland states from New York to California, selling homesites located on the sides of active volcanoes and peddling investments in arid land where the chance of any profitable resale was nil. In most cases, it was a matter of selling fast and leaving town quickly. County auctions for delinquent taxes covered broken promises and supplied a new batch of lots for the next clutch of unsuspecting investors in paradise.

When Hawaii statehood arrived to the noisy salute of cannon on Honolulu's Iolani Palace lawn, Hawaii Island had

Honolulu? Well, oveh deah deeferent, eh? Oveh deah barren, yeah? Too much house. Too much building. You come here you see more trees, yeah? The ocean—I like ocean. Clean, eh. The ocean clean. Yeah, clean air, too. You come here you see more clean, yeah?

John Hale,
Pohoiki, Puna

Time Is on the Side of Nature

no comprehensive zoning ordinance, no general plan, and little county planning authority to prevent individual landowners from changing land uses virtually at will to produce the most profitable return in the shortest time. The arrival of mainland cash in the island spurred speculative buying and selling to unprecedented excesses, in some areas inflating land prices so severely that even today proper development is seriously inhibited and quality, long-range land-use planning by individuals and government is stifled.

Hawaii Governor John Burns first reflected the criticism voiced by numerous civic groups over increasing misuse of limited island land and awareness of growing distress over Hawaii's environmental future. He affirmed, "We have the basic laws on our books to protect and enhance Hawaii's resources of scenic beauty and open spaces." At the same time he cautioned, "Ownership of land does not carry with it the right to deface its natural beauty in the name of progress."

Act 250, Hawaii's statewide zoning law, states its purpose precisely:

> Inadequate controls have caused many of Hawaii's limited and valuable lands to be used for purposes that may have a short-term gain to a few but result in a long-term loss to the income and growth potential of our economy. . . . Scattered subdivisions with expensive, yet reduced, public services; the shifting of prime agricultural lands into non-revenue producing residential uses when other lands are available that could serve adequately the urban needs; failure to utilize fully multiple-purpose lands; these are evidences of the need for public concern and action. Therefore, the legislature finds that in order to preserve, protect and encourage the development of the lands in the state for those uses to which they are best suited for the public welfare . . . the power to zone should be exercised by the state.

The law enjoys broad community support, ranging from large corporate landowners to the Sierra Club and Hawaii Farm Bureau. Only speculative land developers, realtors, and county governments oppose the innovative legislation that strips counties of traditional zoning prerogatives and gives to the state the power to determine boundaries of established communities and stop urban encroachment upon scarce agricultural land, floodplains, and areas of scenic beauty and open space.

Implementation, however, is the key to effective impact of any zoning law upon community growth, and it is in this critical area that Hawaii's controversial land-use law has faltered. It was unfortunate that Burns' financial backers and political advisers did not hold the same ideals and views as the governor. From the beginning, his administration was seriously compromised by the advocates of a harmful "growth is good" policy that consistently interpreted his "open society" concept as a call for unbridled progress and growth.

Mayor Shunichi Kimura of Hawaii County, now a circuit court judge, felt differently, and argued strongly and successfully for slow, quality growth in all segments of the economy. He met the challenges presented by restrictive state zoning laws and land speculators, and created a respected and effective planning department, headed by Raymond Suefuji. Hawaii Island soon showed the way with innovative shoreline setbacks, ordinances to prevent soil erosion in subdivisions, coastal pollution regulations, building height limitations, and a progressive, comprehensive zoning ordinance that included requirements for incremental releases of urban-zoned land based on performance. The Hawaii Island General Plan received a national award for the best plan of its kind at a time when state officials were seriously neglecting overall land-use planning.

In the process of debates and disagreements that received extensive public exposure via newspaper and television coverage, state land-use regulations gradually evolved from a conventional "green-belt" zoning law into a land-use document promising social consequences far beyond the legislature's original intent. The law today is an important tool directing urban growth and protecting irreplaceable scenic resources and wild lands. With appropriate amendments reflecting the growing responsibility of county governments now well staffed with competent planners and armed with strong laws, Hawaii

I think that we should learn to appreciate more the beauty and wonder Hawaii has to offer. I think that if Kane and Kanaloa really did create the oceans I'd have to shake their hands, because they really did a beautiful job with no mistakes.

Rudy Jugoz,
Hilo High School

'Ohi'a lehua in pahoehoe lava, Hawaii Volcanoes National Park

'Ohi'a lehua

will continue to be a national leader in effective land-use legislation. Increasing collaboration among large corporate landowners, developers, and the state and county is already producing restrictive laws that will protect major investments in quality resort facilities and residential subdivisions and at the same time provide incentives to preserve open space of considerable benefit to the general public and the landowner.

In environmental battles, victories often mean empty lots or unobstructed shoreline vistas, soon taken for granted, while defeats are horrendous concrete high-rises, unnecessary highways, and suburban sprawl. The press delights in reporting disaster at great length but seldom features beauty on the front page. The open space that was fought for and won with picket signs and impassioned slogans only a short time before is too soon forgotten by media and activists as the more aggressive developers draw up new projects to pollute the landscape. It is difficult to see victory when the only tangible evidence is open space. Victory for the preservationist is no change that can be noticed. Defeat is a concrete monument where before, all was beauty.

It is perhaps even more difficult to judge the success of zoning ordinances and land-use laws when positive accomplishments include subdivisions and hotels that do not exist because developers were sufficiently prudent not even to begin surveys for an ill-conceived project that would have enraged a concerned community.

The history of Hawaii's struggle to preserve nature's contribution to good living began with the early Hawaiians' own special respect for the land. In later years, local newspapers were replete with stories of continuing public challenges in opposition to blind progress. Hawaii Island officials passed a pioneering ordinance in 1909, making it illegal "in any manner whatsoever to cut, trim, mutilate, destroy or appropriate any shade, ornamental, fruit or other tree growing upon any sidewalk, highway or private property ... without first having permission ... of the Board of Supervisors." The law was enacted primarily to save a lone coconut palm at the junction of Waianuenue and Kamehameha avenues in downtown Hilo. Preservationists lost that one. The electric company decided it was cheaper to push the tree over than move a power pole at the intersection.

Sixty years later, women of the Outdoor Circle mounted a successful boycott of advertisers using the outdoor billboards which were then beginning to proliferate on highways around all the islands. The preservationists won that one.

There are no billboards in Hawaii today.

Citizen activists have played an important role in protecting Hawaii's scenic resources. But the natural beauty that is coveted so highly today by tourist industry and conservationist alike has been saved not so much by courageous politicians and active conservationists as through an unusual combination of obstacles thrown up by nature—volcanic eruptions, tsunami waves, the wilderness of lava fields and tropical jungles—in concert with remnants of feudalistic land ownership. Three-quarters of Hawaii Island is owned by Kamehameha Schools Bishop Estate, corporate sugar plantations, large ranches, and the state of Hawaii. Land monopolies of this magnitude can afford to wait for the opportune time to develop. They are able to invest large sums in elaborate and carefully considered master plans and, perhaps most important, are able to undertake major investments in quality land improvements without demanding immediate payoffs. The result has not been everything a conservationist would desire, and the confrontation between idealist citizen and profit-motivated executive has not always resulted in a positive gain for the land, but by any measure the future must be looked at optimistically, for time is on the side of nature.

Growth as an objective in itself will become less and less a prime consideration in land development when preservation becomes a partner in long-range planning. Establishment of optimum maximum population levels is already part of the planning language. As population growth stabilizes—and it must—the day is not far off when the developer asks himself, "Suppose we just didn't build anything at all?"

These pages are an inventory of our island heritage, the unique scenic environment and natural beauty that has escaped harsh treatment by intruders. The words are those spoken and written by islanders, some of whom claim Hawaii as home or are island born, others of whom are visitors who have recently discovered Hawaii and, like the early Polynesians, may decide to travel no farther.

The photographs reveal the island landscape first seen by exploring Polynesians when they discovered Hawaii over 1,200 years ago. The island seen by Captain Cook when he sailed into Kealakekua Bay nearly 200 years ago. The island excitedly discovered today by thousands of visitors from around the world—an island still surprisingly beautiful after a dozen centuries of human habitation. Most of the surface scars have been touched up by flowers, trees, and fruits brought by im-

I am challenged by the need for giving creative people a place to go to renew themselves. Close to nature, people find a mystical, physical kind of rapport. This is an uplifting, creative environment, and my hotels are designed to keep people as close to nature as possible. . . . These are hotels for self-sufficient people.

Laurance S. Rockefeller,
Owner-builder,
Mauna Kea Beach Hotel

migrants from foreign lands and growing now in a cornucopia of tropical resplendence.

These photographs are of the land, not the people who live on the land, for the island people of today are not unique —they are a neo-Hawaiian family from everywhere. Only the island and its tropical canopy are one of a kind.

The photographs show the land seen by King Kamehameha and his warriors; by missionaries, sugar planters, ranchers, traders; by the residents and visitors who crowd the islands today in increasing numbers; and the land that will be seen by the islanders of tomorrow.

Rather than picture man's effect upon the land, I prefer to display the island I want to remember. The photographs imply the presence of people and their behavior only in part, and then only where use of the land has been gentle and unintrusive. For Hawaii is indeed an island only lightly caressed by people who have lived with the land rather than on it, and who, despite the excesses of a few, have preserved an island lifestyle and an island landscape. These are not the pictures of an island that has been hurt, but of an environment that can still be enjoyed tomorrow.

My Hawaii is photographed not in 1975 or any particular century, but somewhere between the time prehistoric volcanoes thrust a new land from beneath the sea and tomorrow when our children will share this island. Should our concern contribute even slightly toward preserving this land for them, we may earn for ourselves the rare privilege of witnessing our children's delight.

Kamoamoa shore, Kalapana

Hamakua coast

Waipiʻo Valley beach